Language for Banking

Study skills and language practice at advanced level

Francis Radice

Collins ELT
London and Glasgow

Collins ELT
8 Grafton Street
London W1X 3LA

10 9 8 7 6 5 4 3 2 1

First published 1985

Phototypeset by Wyvern Typesetting Ltd, Bristol

Printed in Great Britain by
R. J. Acford

Design by Jacky Wedgwood

ISBN 0 00 370636 2

Acknowledgements

The author and publishers are grateful to the following for
permission to reproduce material in this book (page numbers
given in brackets):

African Business magazine for three tables from the issue of
September 1982 (87, 88); *Asian Finance* magazine for an
article from the issue of 15th September 1982 (86–7);
Associated Examining Board for a question from the GCE O
Level Commerce paper, November 1979 (30); BBC
Publications for part of the index from *Worlds Apart, the
Economic Gulf between Nations* (1971) by Peter Donaldson
(40); Collins Publishers for two extracts from 'The Emergence
of Modern Finance in Europe 1500–1730' by Geoffrey Parker,
in *Fontana Economic History of Europe 1500–1730* (Volume
2) (93–5); Dr S. S. M. Desai for extracts (adapted) from
Rural Banking in India (1979), Himalaya Publishing House,
Bombay (116); Financial Times for the index from *The
Financial Times* of 13th October 1982 (42); The Guardian for
extracts from an article by Peter Rodgers in *The Guardian*
(February 1984) (67); Hodder & Stoughton Educational Ltd
for the contents page (37–8) and exam question (59 (6)) from
Teach Yourself Banking (1981) by Stuart Valentine and Stan
Mason; Institiut Bank-Bank Malaysia for questions from the
Banker's Certificate examination, Stage 1, and the Banking
Diploma examination, Stage 1 (114, 127–8); Institute of
Bankers, London for exam questions (59 (2–4)); Institute of
Bankers in Pakistan for questions from the Banking Diploma
I examination (127–8); Macdonald & Evans Ltd for an extract
from *Banking in India* by K. S. Hasan (118–20); John Murray
Publishers Ltd for exam questions from *Success in Elements
of Banking* (2nd edition, 1983) by David Cox (59 (1)); Martin
Robertson & Co. Ltd for an extract from *Money, Finance and
Development* by P. J. Drake (132–4); *The Oriental Economist*
for three tables from the issue of August 1982 (84, 85);
Overseas Development Institute for part of the contents list
from *Regional Development Banks* by John White (41);
Praeger Publishers Inc., New York, for an extract from
*Development Savings Bank in the Third World – a tool for the
diffusion of economic power* (1983) by Chelliah Loganathan
(130–1); *Standard Chartered Review* for extracts from the
issue of December 1982 (109); Van Nostrand Reinhold (UK)
Ltd, Wokingham, Berkshire, for extracts from *Money: theory,
policy, and institutions* (2nd edition, 1979) by Andrew
Crockett (28–9, 30, 70, 71–2, 76–8); *Your Business* magazine
(57, 59–61).

The author and publishers would also like to thank the
following, who have given permission for illustrations to be
reproduced:

The Australian Banker magazine (44, 54, 56, 75); *The
Bankers Magazine* (Boston), © Warren, Gorham & Lamont
Inc., 210 South Street, Boston, Massachusetts (46, 127); B. T.
Batsford Ltd (21); Collins Publishers for the map from 'The
Emergence of Modern Finance in Europe 1500–1730' by
Geoffrey Parker, in *Fontana Economic History of Europe
1500–1730* (Volume 2) (91); Gemeentearchief Amsterdam
(101); The Mansell Collection (18); Methuen & Co. Ltd for
illustrations from *A Survey of Primitive Money* (1949) by
A. H. Quiggin (8, 11); *Your Business* magazine for cartoons
by Hunt (57, 60).

Every effort has been made to contact the owners of
copyright material produced in this book, but in some cases
this has not been possible. The publishers apologise for any
omission, and if details are sent, will be glad to rectify these
when the title is reprinted.

Author's acknowledgements

I have received practical help with research from staff at the
Institute of Bankers in London, Karachi, Bombay, Lagos,
Kuala Lumpur and Broadwater College, London. I have also
benefited from facilities to develop and teach the course from
students, English teachers and staff at the Centre of Business
Studies, Greenwich and the North London Tuition Centre. I
should also mention the personal encouragement I was given
by Brian Rawle and Jim Davie of the Institute of Bankers,
Hal Stuart, Charlotte Coudrille, who typed much of the
course, Dr Kenneth Cripwell of the Institute of Education,
University of London, the editorial staff of Collins and my
wife and children who put up with, and supported me
throughout.

Contents

Introduction to teachers

This course is intended for students who have used English for a number of years, possibly as a medium in secondary school, and are interested in, or have to take exams on, banking and finance. Their oral English is probably much more advanced than their reading and writing ability. Also the students may know more about the subject than you, but your curiosity will serve as a genuine motive for getting students to talk about banking.

For these reasons it is important for you to take an interest in banking and read one or two textbooks. The most readable is *Teach Yourself Banking*, by Stuart Valentine and Stan Mason, Teach Yourself Books (paperback), Hodder and Stoughton, 1981. But you should read the introductory textbook recommended for the students' course and, in order to get an idea of the problems (i.e. of dryness, textual density and ethno-centrism) faced by your students, one or two of the other recommended textbooks. There is also a list at the end of this introduction.

The language and study skills elements of this course are partly based on the 'top-down processing' principle (which has its roots in Gestalt psychology). The idea is that it is easier to learn about a subject if you survey the whole of it at the start and work your way down to the details later. This also applies to grammar, in that the student is more encouraged by a situation where the lower rank problems are dealt with after the higher rank ones.

The way you use this course depends very much on your teaching situation, the number and background of your students and their preferred learning style. On the whole, instructions such as 'work in pairs', 'group work' and 'prepare for the next lesson' have been omitted, since you are in the best position to decide when such techniques should be applied in your particular situation. In general, the activities should be carried out in the order in which they appear and it is important that students should try to answer questions even though it is difficult, if not impossible, to decide on the answers. In the **Preparing to read** sections the questions are posed, in many cases, *before* the answers are known. The aim is to teach students to frame their own questions before approaching a study task.

How to use this course:

Proceed in short sessions of 5–10 minutes each in which students are working together as a class, in groups, in pairs, or silently on their own. Vary the way you work as much as possible.

You should require some written answers, particularly for the **Self-assessment** sections, and these should be taken into account for continuous assessment. The fewer periods per week you have at your disposal, the more written answers are necessary.

Students should get into the habit of correcting their own answers as soon as possible after they have been written. But it is very important that students understand that the value of the course comes mainly through solving and understanding problems and not simply from knowing the answers.

Six sections recur regularly in the units. Each requires its own distinctive approach. It will help both you and your students if you are clear about the teaching intentions of each of these sections.

Preview

Use the list of items to clarify what the unit is going to deal with. Students may not understand the whole list, which is intended more for your guidance than theirs. But it is important that they should understand the reasons for each part of the course before doing it.

Make sure they distinguish at least the three areas: content, language work and study aids.

Preparing to read

The purpose of this section is to make students aware that they should use their existing knowledge and organising ability to help them in all reading tasks. Do not insist on all questions being answered. They should, however, be explored and discussed either in groups or by the whole class.

Subject Talk as little as possible here. The students should talk as much as possible about what they know about a subject before discussing it. Encourage them to formulate their own questions on what they want to know about a topic. Questions that no one knows the answer to should be written in notebooks to be answered later.

Coverage Students should refer to content lists of their banking textbooks, which should be brought to the English class. Have a look at the coverage of banking in the index of an encyclopaedia to get an idea of maximum coverage. This will help you elicit yes/no answers on selected items.

Organisation Many students find organisation frames obvious when presented with them but are unable to devise ones for themselves. To help them transpose texts into diagrams, draw organisation frameworks of well-known news-items or stories as examples and let them practise creating examples of these. Note that tabulated diagrams are not the only way in which texts can be represented. (See pp. 113 and 114.)

Purpose Students should analyse different kinds of *writer purpose*, e.g. as in advertising, notices, letters. Discuss different kinds of information. Bring short examples for study, e.g. leaflets such as those displayed in banks, letters, and notices.

To avoid complication, the *reader's purpose* is not included in the first presentation of SCOPE in Unit 1 but is dealt with in Unit 6.

Illustrated examples Discuss the function of all the illustrations. Some of the illustrations included in the course have the dual purpose of entertainment and illustration of a point. Others (such as graphs) are used to provide information in digestible form.

The passage

The reading texts are, with the exception of those of Units 1 and 2, on the same levels of difficulty as those of banking textbooks, but they deal with social, historical and political aspects of banking which are not normally covered in banking courses. The aim is not to simplify the task by providing purpose-written texts, but to present stimulating but closely related topics and a step-by-step procedure for handling the difficulties in them. The reading passages, however, use the vocabulary of finance extensively, in contexts different from those of the students' courses. The questions in the margin should be worked through after the passage has been read and understood. They are intended to highlight the way the parts of a text are related to each other and how different expressions signal what is to follow.

Procedure   Follow the steps described in the rubric. Adopt a problem-solving approach. Avoid giving direct answers but show the students how they can arrive at the answers themselves, either by reading further in the text and guessing creatively or by discussion with other students. Dictionaries should be used as a last resort.

Sense groups   (Unit 10) After the text has been studied silently, read out the section with marked sense groups, pausing at the marks. The rules for making these pauses are not absolute. As far as possible, they should sound natural and consist of one 'unit of meaning' at phrase level. While you are reading, the students should mark the pauses. Let them mark the remainder of the passage. Then go through the results jointly. Discuss any differences with a view to clarifying the structures of the sentences concerned.

Discussion

In the **Ask and answer** sections make sure every student has a turn. Start by getting a volunteer to pose a question and then choose someone to answer it. It is essential that *the students should choose* the person they want to answer their questions, with the rider that someone who hasn't answered a question already should be chosen. Avoid stepping in to correct a mistaken answer. The responsibility for monitoring the answers should be the students'. Your function should be to monitor their monitoring of the answers. The person who answers must then pose the next question.

Note that certain types of question follow each other naturally:
    What are the advantages to banks of long-term loans?
    Any other advantages?
    Anything else?
These elliptical questions can be used when several or a whole series of answers is possible. Students should be encouraged to exhaust all possibilities with such questions. Also it should not be assumed that the reading passage is the only place where the answer can be found. You should encourage students to give expression to their general or specialised knowledge on the subject.

Analysis

This section deals with grammatical points that arise in the texts. It is bound to be selective. The items have been chosen for their usefulness in writing essays and exam answers on banking. They were also selected to deal with common errors. But you should also be on the look-out for other grammatical problems. These should be identified by reading through the essays written for the banking subject lecturers, not just the English 'general interest' essays. The English teacher should study the requirements of the subject tutors in terms of language, because the aim of the English course should be to facilitate the professional studies rather than merely practise independent and unrelated skills.

Procedure Let the students provide answers orally. Then ask them to write down some examples. If they appear to be writing the sentences 100% correctly, there is no need for all the examples to be written out. If you ask the students to write out the examples in their own time, it is important that they do the corrections in the following session. As a rule, spelling and lexical mistakes can be rewritten individually. Grammatical mistakes should be corrected by the whole sentence being rewritten.

Extension

This section deals with skills of direct relevance to the study of banking, including note-making, vocabulary extension, asking and answering questions on the topic and understanding the logical organisation of texts. If you are short of time, this section can be set for private study but it should be checked and a record kept of results.

Self-assessment

This section is more for the students to use as a check on their own progress than for the teacher. It should be possible, with mature students, to assign self-assessment entirely to them, as written work, and only check on the students' own results. If you show that you trust them to mark themselves honestly, the tendency for individuals to raise their own marks should die out.

LANGUAGE FOR BANKING is meant to be of *direct help* to students in their efforts to study banking and finance in English, whichever country they are in. The main emphasis is on banking for development. It is hoped that the subjects introduced will provide inspiration for further discussion of economic problems which are of particular interest to the students and will, among other things, lead to improved communication in English. As such, it is not merely an English course, but a means of broadening the students' interest in banking, and making their study of it more effective.

Books on banking

McRae, H. and Cairncross, F., *Capital City: London as a Financial Centre* (2nd edition), Magnum Books, 1985
Hanson, D. G., *Service Banking*, Institute of Bankers, London, 1979
Sampson, Anthony, *The Money Lenders*, Hodder and Stoughton, 1981

Basic textbooks

Cox, D., *Success in Elements of Banking*, John Murray, 1979
Perry, F. E., *The Elements of Banking* (3rd edition), Methuen/Institute of Bankers, 1977

All the above are available in paperback.

Unit 1

Commodity money

Bronze cannon used as money in Borneo.

Preview

In this unit you will

1 survey a passage before reading it

2 guess the meaning of some words

3 tabulate information from a passage

4 decide whether nouns used in writing are singular or plural

5 revise some aspects of punctuation

6 decide when to use *the* before nouns in writing

7 see how certain tenses are used in exposition texts

8 learn some useful words for banking purposes

9 discuss the content of the passage by asking and answering questions about it

You will also be able to check your own progress in the **Self-assessment** section at the end of the unit.

Preparing to read

**Ask questions first.
Find answers later**

A Before reading think about the full *scope* of the text. Remember SCOPE because it also stands for Subject, Coverage, Organisation, Purpose and Examples.

B It may not be possible to answer the questions below without reading the text in detail. But it is important to formulate questions about what you are going to read even before you know the answers. This will help you assimilate the material.

See how many of the following questions you can answer by not reading the passage in detail but by using the strategies listed in the box immediately below. (The strategies will be dealt with again later in this course.) The questions you cannot answer can be left to answer during or after your reading.

Possibly find the answer by:

– quickly running your eyes over the whole text

– looking for key words or headings

– thinking about the meaning of the title

– having a quick look at the illustrations

– looking for titles, names, figures or quoted material

– discussing the subject with someone else

– reading the first and last sentences

Any other strategies?

1 The subject What is the subject about?

    a the way objects have been used as money
    b shells and ornaments used as money
    c the qualities and uses of money
    d goods traded for money

2 The coverage How much of the subject does it cover?

    a economic uses of money
    b economic and social uses of money
    c mainly social uses of money
    d countries of origin of different kinds of money
    e b + c
    f b + c + d

3 The organisation How is the text organised? Study the diagram below. It shows one way of looking at the structure or organisation of the text. Complete as many spaces in the last two columns as you can without reading the text in detail.

Functions of money	social functions	Qualities of money	convenient	*examples*
			attractive	
			acceptable	
	economic functions			

4 The writer's purpose Does the writer want to

    a tell a story?
    b explain a subject?

5 Illustrated examples What sort of information do the drawings give? Information about

    a the uses of money
    b the origins of money
    c the appearance of money
    d all of these

The passage *Commodity money*

A   Read the passage and look at the drawings quickly to understand the gist of the text.

B   Then read the passage more slowly.

C   Read the passage again, answering the questions on the left.

D   Some of the questions are about things *not in the text*. You should answer them by
– using your own knowledge of the subject,
– asking a fellow student, or by
– looking them up in a textbook or dictionary.

Key expressions are in **bold** type.

Numbers in brackets refer to lines in the text.

1 Find two words (4 and 6) which have roughly the same meaning as *function* (4).

2 What are the four economic functions of money? (The answer is *not* in the text.)

3 *limited* (9) = increased? opened? restricted?

4 Which of these functions seem to be the simplest?

5 *various* (18) = many? strange? different?

6 *portable* (20) = easy to _____

7 *combined* (20) = mixed up? joined together? took advantage of?

8 *origin* (25) = where the money _____ from

9 Money having two uses would be called dual-_____ money.

Any object that is used as money may be called commodity money. But in order to understand a money object more clearly, we should ask, 'What was it used for?' If we answer this question, we will **discover the function** or purpose of
5   the money object.

Nowadays the uses of money are mostly economic. There are **four economic functions** which are usually given in the beginnings of elementary textbooks on banking or commerce. But in the past the use of money was not limited
10   to these four economic functions. There were **other equally important functions** which were **social**, **religious**, **magical** or simply **decorative**. Sometimes the economic function was **specialised** and restricted to buying slaves or paying the bride price. We should try to understand those people
15   and their money objects as they were, and not from the point of view of modern economic functions of money.

In addition to the functions of money, we should look at **its qualities**. What were the various forms of money like? Were they light? heavy? countable? decorative? beautiful?
20   useful? portable? hard to get? Perhaps they combined some of these qualities. But one thing is certain. They were fully **acceptable as payment** which could be used to make further payments, otherwise they could not be called money.

25   Finally, it is of interest to note the **country of origin** of the money and the **extent of the area where it was acceptable**. Was it special-purpose local money? Or was it general-purpose regional money?

Examples of commodity money

The following drawings show different forms of money. Decide on and list the functions and characteristics of each one. You will be discussing these in the section that follows.

1 *Bronze cannon used as money in Borneo – ornamental value – used especially for bride-price and the purchase of slaves*

5 *Chung ch'ien or 'bell cash' – considered to have magical value – used as marriage gifts in China during the Han period – an example of special purpose money*

8 *Gold rings, Mycenae, Ancient Greece – different values made by different numbers of rings fixed together*

2 *Cowries from New Guinea on a loosely knotted string – convenient for paying out shells*

6 *Cattle, Roman Britain – used to pay blood-money – Roman Law compensation: for breaking the bones of a free man 300 donkeys, a slave's bones 150 donkeys, 25 donkeys for hitting a free man*

9 *Brass ornaments, Indonesia*

3 *A New Guinea conus shell necklace – a useful way to carry small change*

10 *Rice – used as a measure of value in Japan*

4 *Flying fox jaws, Fiji – used for peace-making ceremonies – worn as a sign of peace – useful as a purse*

7 *Iron bar, Nigeria – widely used for trade – also turned into hoes – in 1934 1 bar = 1 penny*

11 *Bronze axe-head used for trade in bronze-age Germany*

Discussion

Ask and answer

A   Ask and answer questions with your fellow students, using questions like the ones below. Do not wait long for an answer. If the person you ask cannot answer your question, ask another student.

1 As you ask and answer, complete the **Functions** column of the table below:

What were *axe-heads* used for?
They were used for *payments in trade*.

What else could they be used for?
They could be used for *making wood-choppers*.

What else could . . .

What could *Chinese bells* be used for?
They could be used for *magic*.

Ask about the other money objects.

Form of money	Functions	Qualities	Country of origin
Axe-heads	medium of exchange useful tool	useful, valuable, heavy	Bronze-Age Germany
Brass ornaments			
Cowries			
Cows			
Rice			
Gold rings			
Fox-bat jaws			
Conus shells			
Bell cash			
Bronze cannon	store of value		
Iron bars			

2 Now, as you ask and answer, complete the **Qualities** column above:

What are *axe-heads* like as money?
They are *useful*, *valuable* and *heavy*.

What else are they like?

3 Now ask and answer questions for the **Country of origin** column.

4 Now ask and answer any remaining questions of your own.

B Advanced discussion In groups discuss the following. Then report on your conclusions to the whole class.

1 For the purposes of economic analysis, the only correct view of commodity money is one which analyses its economic functions only.

2 It is impossible to consider any form of money outside the context of the society in which it was used.

NOTE   It may be easier to postpone discussing the next two questions until after doing the **Extension** section of this unit.

3 Commodity money has certain advantages which modern bank notes do not have. There may be some situations in which it is better to have commodities than modern money.

4 Some of the forms of commodity money have many of the qualities of money – for instance, convenience, acceptability and accountability – and some of its modern economic functions. But none of the forms of commodity money have all the qualities and all the functions that money should have. Is this true?

Analysis

Using 'the'

A Compare the two paragraphs below. The subject matter is nearly the same. What is the difference between them?

The coins in the till
The coins in the till were made in the Royal Mint which is the government factory where official coins are made. The highest value coin in the UK is the £1 piece.

Official coinage
Coins in tills are made in mints which are government factories where official coins are made. High value coins are not very common.

B Discuss the following:

1 Why is *the* used in the paragraph on the left?

2 Why is *the* not used in the paragraph on the right?

In your discussion talk about the following:
  particular meaning, generalisations, singular/plural

C Conclusions about the use of *the*: Which of these statements are correct?

1 Sometimes it is wrong to use *the*.
2 You can use *the* whenever you like in front of a noun.
3 It is quite good to use *the* sometimes.
4 Whether you use *the* or not is important because it affects the meaning of what you write.
5 Sometimes the use of *the* is compulsory.

D   Practice using 'the' Sometimes the use of *the* is optional. Rewrite the following correct paragraph without the *the*s:

The banks in Britain are well distributed in the high streets of every town. Even the small towns and some of the large villages have banks. But the names of the banks do not vary a great deal. The hundreds of banks that existed long ago have been amalgamated into the four huge companies.

E   Rewrite the following incorrect paragraphs, inserting *the* where it is needed:

1 Currency of Afghanistan is afghani. (People are called Afghans.) Before invasion, afghanis could be bought and sold freely in Kabul market. Before buying currency, money-changer would tell you his price. If you wanted, you could go to next money-changer to try and get a better price.

2 Social uses of money nowadays are indirect. Rich show size of their bank accounts by display of expensive possessions. Display of possessions is also used to hide small size of bank accounts of people who would like to look rich.

F   Further discussion Go through the Reading Passage and, with the help of your teacher, decide why *the* is used in each case.

Singular or plural

A   Look at these examples from the passage:

Any object that [1]is used as money may be called commodity money. But we should ask 'What [2]was [3]it used for?'
Nowadays the uses of money [4]are mostly economic. There are four economic functions which [5]are usually given in the beginnings of elementary textbooks on banking or commerce. But in the past the use of money [6]has not been limited to these four economic functions.

B   Notice these important connections in paragraph A
1 *is* must be singular because *any object* is singular.
2 *was* must be singular because *any object* is singular.
3 *it* must be singular because *any object* is singular.
4 *are* must be plural because the phrase *the uses* is plural.
5 *are* is plural because it refers to *functions*.
6 *has* is singular because it refers to *the use*.

C   Practice: Write down the correct form of each of the pairs of words in the paragraph below:

Sea shells (1 is/are) well known (2 example/examples) of commodity money. (3 It/They) (4 is/are) usually mentioned in textbooks about money. In many (5 way/ways) (6 this/these) local (7 form/forms) of money (8 do/does) not serve the modern economic purposes of money. But a local money object (9 has/have) an important social function in addition to an economic use. So it is meaningless to criticise local forms of money if (10 it/they) (11 does/do) not serve as convenient (12 unit/units) of exchange in an industrial society. A string of shells used to have more value on some Pacific islands than a fifty dollar bill.

Punctuation

A   Look at how commas are used to divide a sentence into main clause and subordinate clause or phrase:

In order to understand a money object more clearly,
we should ask what it is used for.

If we answer this question,
we will discover the function or purpose of the money object.

We should try to understand those people and their money objects as they were,
and not from the point of view of modern economic functions of money.

B   Rewrite the following sentences, inserting one comma in each, in the same way:

1 The acceptability of commodity money depends on the value of the money object while the acceptability of modern money depends on habit.

2 Although trade can be carried on without money some form of medium of exchange makes trade easier.

3 The social aspects of money should be considered if one wants to form an adequate idea of what money is.

4 Apart from their ornamental value bronze cannon were used specially for paying bride-price and buying slaves.

Use of the past tense

A   Notice that for describing present-day systems in banking the present tense is used:

examples . . . the uses of money are mostly economic.
            There are four economic functions . . .
            What are the various forms of money like?

B   Sometimes you need to switch to using the past. The writer has done this in paragraph 2 of the Reading Passage. Why? Which phrase requires the past tense?

C   Study the examples again. Then rewrite the following paragraph, putting the verbs shown in brackets into the past or present tense:

Bank notes (come) into use during the seventeenth century in Europe. Despite this fact, coins (be) still in greater demand than notes in 1914. At the outbreak of the First World War, the value of coins in circulation in Britain (be) £160 million, while notes (total) only £40 million. This situation (change) only when the Treasury (withdraw) gold from circulation. However, bank deposits (remain) the most important form of money since they (amount to) £1,000 million. This figure now (stand) at over £49,000 million and the ratio of coins and notes to deposits (be) much smaller.

Extension

Vocabulary

A   Note how the following words are used in the Reading Passage. Numbers in brackets refer to lines in the passage:

limited (9)
specialised (13)
restricted (13)
combined (20)
country of origin (25)

B   Now use the words to complete the following sentences:

1 Some banks are _____ and concentrate on providing only certain financial services.

2 The use to which we can put the money has been _____ by our bank to buying spare parts and training services for the equipment.

3 The manager _____ our overdraft to £500.

4 For political reasons, many countries are interested in the _____ of the goods they import.

5 The goods are to be shipped by road and sea under a _____ transport document.

Converting notes into text

A   This exercise has two purposes:

1 to show how notes may be made so that you can make them for yourself later in this course
2 to give practice in writing well-formed sentences

B   Study the notes under the drawings of commodity money objects (p. 11) and write mini-paragraphs like the following:

1 Bronze cannon were used as money in Borneo. They had ornamental value and were used especially for paying bride-price and purchasing slaves.

2 Cowries from New Guinea were kept on a loosely knotted string. They were convenient for paying out single shells.

NOTE   1   You have to insert verbs to make complete sentences.
       2   You can write either *used for the purchase of* . . . or *used for purchasing* . . .

Tabulating information

A   Study the tables on pages 9 and 12 and the way their sections are related to the key phrases in the passage.

1 What are the advantages of each table?
2 What are the disadvantages of each table?

B   Discuss the tables as ways of writing notes and revising information before exams.

Self-assessment

A   Answer the questions below. Do not refer back to the unit. When you have finished, check your answers in the Answer Key at the end of the book.

marks

1 How can you usefully survey a text before reading it?   (1)

2 What three sources of information should you consult to help you understand what you are reading if the answer is not in the text?   (3)

3 Why might the economic explanation of money alone be unsatisfactory?   (2)

4 Rewrite the following sentences. Insert the word *the* where necessary. Choose the singular or plural form of the words in brackets:

Notes which we now carry (is/are) worth no more than paper (it/they) (is/are) printed on. Sentence on note saying 'I promise to pay bearer sum of one pound' only (mean/means) you can exchange it for another pound note.   (10)

5 Rewrite the following. Insert commas where necessary. Put the verbs shown in brackets into the correct tense:

Until quite recently even though paper money (be) more convenient coins (remain) more popular.   (3)

6 Complete the following sentences with one word each:

a Recently our government has _____ our freedom to take money out of the country.   (1)

b The amount you are allowed to take out is _____ to £4,000.   (1)

7 Rewrite the following notes in well-formed sentences:

iron bar currency used for trade – also turned into hoes – in 1934
1 bar = 1 penny Nigeria   (4)

B   After checking your answers, award yourself marks out of a total of 25.

Unit 2   Coin currency

*A late sixteenth-century
goldsmith banker*

Preview

In this unit you will learn to

1 think about what you know about the subject of a passage before reading it

2 understand some directly stated information in the text

3 understand how pronouns are used to bind texts together

4 understand how texts are bound together by certain kinds of meanings

5 ask and answer questions about the advantages and disadvantages of coinage

6 put the main verb in the correct position in certain sentences

7 use verbs in the passive

8 practise using certain kinds of adjectives

9 discuss the advantages and disadvantages of coin currency

You will be able to check your progress in the **Self-assessment** section at the end of the unit.

Preparing to read

Surveying the subject

A   What do you know about coins? Prepare to read the passage by surveying the subject, to recall what you already know about coin currency.

B   Use your knowledge of coins to ask and answer questions. For example:

1 What are coins?

They are . . .
(pieces of metal, small, used as money, low/high value, metal . . .)

2 What are coins like?

They are . . .
(flat, disc-shaped, useful . . .)

3 What can they be used for?
Any other uses?

They can be used for . . .
(shopping . . .)

4 What metals are they made of?

5 What do coins usually have on their sides?

(heads, symbols, figures . . .)

6 What sort of symbols do coins usually have?

7 What symbols do the coins of your country have on them?

The passage   *Coin currency*

A   Read the passage through quickly to understand the gist of it.

B   Read the passage again more slowly. The alternative meanings of the words on the left are given to help you arrive at a *more accurate meaning*, though you may know the word already.

C   Answer the questions on the left.

Numbers in brackets refer to lines in the text.

1 *Longest history* compared to what?

2 *currency* (9) = commodity money? national money? money objects?

3 *circulation* (10) = trade? going round among the people? going round in circles?

4 *universal* (13) = of the universe? world-wide? general?

Coins are the best-known form of money. They have the longest history (nearly 3,000 years) and have been more widely accepted as payment than any other form of commodity money. In the past, particularly, this has been true
5   of coins made of precious metals such as the Maria Theresa thaler. This is a 200-year-old silver coin. It shows the head of the Austrian empress and was acceptable as payment in some Middle Eastern countries until only a few years ago. Another example of currency which was once in inter-
10   national circulation is the coins of Alexander the Great and other Greek kings. These were used 2,300 years ago in countries as far apart as India and Italy.

The popularity and universal acceptability of some coin money is easy to understand. Coins are solid, attractive,

5 Are these examples of
functions or are they *qualities*?

6 *symbols* (17) = signs? musical
instruments? names?

7 *denominations* (26) =
amounts? symbols? names?

15 hard-wearing and easy to handle. The head of the ruler of the country shown on them confirms their value as the official medium of exchange. Coins also depict symbols of the country and government which give law and order to the people. These increase confidence and are therefore
20 helpful to shopkeepers and merchants. For them, peace and a sound currency are important.

In addition to the qualities mentioned above, coinage can be produced in a wide range of values. For shopping and purchase of small items, small coins of base metals
25 such as lead, copper or tin can be used. Coins of larger denominations can be made of silver or gold.

D   Write down the answers to the following as quickly as possible:

marks

1 How long is the history of coinage?
   a 2,300 years
   b 200 years
   c nearly 3,000 years   (1)

2 Which coinage was accepted until quite recently? That of:
   a Alexander the Great
   b Maria Theresa
   c the Greek kings   (1)

3 Which of the following statements is true according to the passage?
   a All coins are accepted as payment internationally.
   b Only precious metal coins are widely acceptable.
   c Certain coins have had international acceptance.   (1)

4 List three reasons for the popularity and universal acceptability of some coin money.   (3)

5 What features of coinage are helpful to shopkeepers and merchants?   (2)

6 What feature of coins shows they are the official medium of exchange?   (1)

7 What sort of coins are useful for measuring small values?
   a base metal coins
   b precious metal coins
   c larger denominations   (1)
                                                          Total (10)

E   Check your answers with the Answer Key. How much did you score? Keep a record of your score and percentage mark.

Discussion

A sixteenth-century mint

A Study the pictures of the late sixteenth-century goldsmith banker (p. 18) and the mint where coins are being made (left). Then answer the questions.

1 What differences are there between this bank of 400 years ago and a modern bank with regard to **a** security? **b** acceptability of the medium of exchange and **c** payment?

2 The picture shows a sixteenth-century mint where coins were forged and struck.
  a What was debasement of the coinage?
  b What economic problems did it cause?
  c Can you think of any other problems relating to coin money?

Check your answers in the Answer Key.

B Ask and answer questions as follows:

What are the advantages of coin money?   Coins are light.
What other advantages are there?
Any other advantages?
What are the disadvantages of coin money? Some coins are too heavy.
What other disadvantages are there?
Any other disadvantages?

Ask your fellow students other questions of your own.

Analysis

Connecting words

A Study the ways in which the sentences in the text over the page are bound together.

B **Pronouns referring back to previous words and phrases** Study the examples on lines 1, 5, 6, 7, 10, 11, 17, 20 and 21 (in the passage) of *they*, *this*, *it*, *which*, *these* and *them*.

C Now, from this list, supply one word for each space in the paragraph below to complete the sense. Write down your answers:

In many ways, coins have been the most useful form of money. (1)_____ can be made in small as well as large denominations. Well-known examples of (2)_____ are the gold sovereign and the farthing, (3)_____ was a quarter of a penny. But neither of (4)_____ are used any more and the reasons for (5)_____ are interesting. The farthing's purchasing power is too small. (6)_____ simply won't buy anything. The gold sovereign, on the other hand, has gone out of use because (7)_____ is worth too much and its market value changes independently of its monetary face value.

1 pronoun referring back

2 pronoun referring back

3 *silver* (7), an example of *precious metals* (5–6)

4 an example of *in the past* (5)

5 *currency* (10) = *coins* (1)

6 *which* (10)

7 *international* (10), an explanation of *widely accepted* (3)

8 *ruler* (16), *kings* (11), *empress* (8) go together

9 *countries far apart* (12) = *international* (10)

10 *government* (19) goes with *the ruler* (16) and *law and order* (19)

11 *peace* (21) = *law and order* (19)

12 *base metals* (24) goes with *precious metals* (5–6)

13 The *thaler* (6) is an example of a *denomination* (25)

Coins are the best-known form of money. They have the longest history (nearly 3,000 years) and have been more widely accepted as payment than any other form of commodity money.

5   In the past, this has been true of coins made of precious metals such as the Maria Theresa thaler. This is a 200-year-old silver coin. It shows the head of the Austrian empress and was acceptable as payment in some Middle Eastern countries until only a few years ago. Another example of
10   currency which was in international circulation is the coins of Alexander the Great and other Greek kings. These were used 2,300 years ago in countries as far apart as India and Italy.

The popularity and universal acceptability of some coin
15   money is easy to understand. Coins are solid, attractive, hard-wearing and easy to handle. The head of the ruler of the country on them confirms their value as the official medium of exchange. Coins also depict symbols of the country and government which give law and order to the
20   people. These are helpful to shopkeepers and merchants. For them peace and a good currency are important.

In addition to the qualities mentioned above, coinage can be produced in a wide range of values. For shopping and purchase of small items, small coins of base metals
25   such as lead, copper or tin can be used. Larger denominations can be made of silver or gold.

Word families

A Look at the examples which show how words belonging to the same family link sentences to each other. They are on the lines 1, 5–6, 6, 7, 10, 14, 16, 19, 25 and 26 of the passage.

B Draw the family trees below and complete them with words from the passage.

1

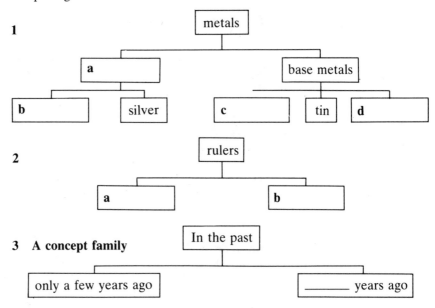

2

3   A concept family

C Study the paragraph and the family tree diagram below. Use the words from the diagram and the paragraph to complete blanks 1–4. Write down the answers:

When England was a Roman colony (1)_____ and (2)_____ were used to assess damage for murder or injury. The value of (3)_____ has also been appreciated in other places. In New Guinea, for much of its history, pigs have been the highest form of wealth.

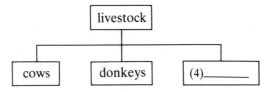

D Write down the missing words of the following paragraph and draw the diagram, completing it with one word for each space:

The amount of blood money fixed for fines in Roman Britain depended on the social rank of the injured person, and only partly on the seriousness of the (1)_____ . For instance the fine for hitting a free man was 20 donkeys but for (2)_____ the (3)_____ of a slave it was only 10 donkeys. For accidentally killing a slave, the blood money was less than the fine for breaking the arm of a free citizen.

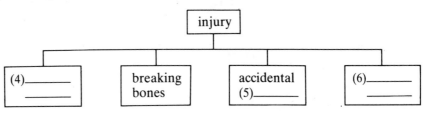

Connecting words: sets

A   Look at these words from the text: *peace, law and order*, and *government*. Notice how they are related.

B   Then read the list of expressions below and notice which words relate to each other:

receiver, bandit, cash-register, gallop, security, assistant, goods, rider, saddle-bag, extension, number, shelf-space, prevention, display, robbery, shop

C   Now write down the four headings below and group the above words under appropriate headings.

1   Retail business   **2**   Telephoning   **3**   Horsemanship   **4**   Crime

D   You have now made four *sets*. Each set may be extended to include other terms related to the main topic. Now, from the above lists of expressions, supply one word for each space in the following paragraph:

The Chinese called their paper notes 'flying money' because it could travel much faster than coin. A (1)_____ with a (2)_____ full of paper could make his horse (3)_____ away from a (4)_____ much more easily with notes than if he was carrying coins. This shows that the development of money has been strongly influenced by the need for (5)_____ in a world where there is a lot of (6)_____ .

E   Which of the four set headings above have you used?

Connecting words: equivalences

These are expressions which do not have exactly the same meaning but, for the writer's purposes, may be taken as *equivalent*, or having the same value.

A   Study the following examples in the passage on p. 22. (Line numbers are shown in brackets.) You will see that *more widely accepted . . . than any other form of commodity money* (2–3) is equivalent to *best-known form of money* (1) and has the effect of binding the text together. In this way the third sentence is linked to the second sentence.

currency (10)	equivalent to	*coins* (1)
more widely accepted (2–3)	equivalent to	*in international circulation* (10)
the ruler (16)	equivalent to	*government* (19)

B   Now match the expressions in the column on the left with their equivalents in the column on the right:

1 safe deposit	**a** money
2 personal adornment	**b** secure asset
3 agricultural implements	**c** jewellery
4 medium of exchange	**d** farm tools
5 store of value	**e** strong room

Using verbs

A   Study the structure of the sentences in the table below:

	Subject	Verb	
1	Coins	were	everywhere.
2	Greek coins	were	everywhere.
3 After Alexander's conquest of the Persian empire	Greek coins	were accepted	everywhere from India to Italy.
4	Dealings	were suspended	everywhere.
5	Exchange dealings	were suspended	in the markets.
6 Following the dollar crisis	exchange dealings	were suspended	in the markets everywhere.
7	Greek coins	were accepted	everywhere following Alexander's conquest of the Persian empire.
8	Exchange dealings	were suspended	in the markets everywhere following the dollar crisis.

B   Rewrite the following sentences, inserting the main verb in the correct form. Put the verb after the subject phrase as shown in the table:

1 Because of the value of gold and silver these metals to mint money (use)
2 A new cheque book with my name in it as soon as I had opened the account (issue)
3 A system of payment by bank cards in one town in France (try out)
4 After the purchase has been completed a card into the shopkeeper's machine (insert)
5 Several machines in shops which had agreed to participate in the experiment (fit)
6 Some years ago a similar experiment in California whereby customers paid for their goods in supermarkets by inserting bank cards into machines (try out)
7 With this system if your account is overdrawn your bank card in the shop in front of other people (reject)
8 Because of the embarrassment caused by such incidents the system by the public (not accept)
9 The scheme and people went back to using credit cards cheques and cash (withdraw)

Extension

Word study

A   Study the way the following phrases are used in the reading passage 'Coin currency' (pp. 19–20). Numbers refer to lines in the passage:

well known   *the best-known* (1)
widely-accepted (3)   the most widely accepted
hard-wearing (15)   the most hard-wearing

B   Now use phrases from the lists above to improve the following paragraph:

Credit cards as a method of payment are in the USA. Made from a form of plastic they fit easily into a wallet or pocket of a handbag. The cards are all over the world.

C   Continue the paragraph about credit cards using the following:

specially designed, well thought out, clearly printed

Self-assessment

A   Answer the questions below without looking back at the previous pages:

marks

1 What should you do about the subject of a text before reading?   (1)

2 Why should you read a passage through quickly at first?   (2)

3 *Fruit*, *apples*, *pears*, *bananas* is an example of
  a a word family   **b** a set   **c** equivalence   (1)

4 *Cheque*, *bank*, *account*, *cashier* is an example of
  a a word family   **b** a set   **c** equivalence   (1)

5 Why are pronouns important in texts?
  a They refer back to previous words.
  b They are used instead of nouns.
  c They make sentences shorter.   (1)

6 Which of the following are advantages of coins for modern purposes?
  a Their weight can be increased to any size.
  b They can be produced in small denominations.
  c They are hard-wearing.
  d Gold coins have a very long history.   (4)

7 Rewrite the following, inserting the main verbs (which are shown in brackets) in the correct forms:
  a The machines in the French shops in much the same way as cash points outside banks in Britain. (operate)   (2)
  b After the cash card has been inserted, the personal number from memory on the machine's keyboard. (type)   (2)

8 Improve each of these sentences by inserting an adjective phrase from the passage:
  a Metals are usually used to mint coins.   (2)
  b Dollars are for payment in international trade.   (2)

9 Write down one advantage and one disadvantage of coins made of precious metals.   (2)

Total (20)

B   Now check your answers in the Answer Key. Make a note of your mark and percentage.

C   If you gave the wrong answers for any questions, try to understand why you went wrong and the reasons for the correct answers.

Unit 3   Money in modern economics

Preview

In this unit you will learn to

1 use notes as a preparation to understand a text

2 distinguish between intrinsic and extrinsic properties of money

3 understand the basis of the monetary system

4 distinguish between directly and indirectly stated information

5 apply outside knowledge to understanding the text

6 pick out the main verbs in sentences in the passage

7 write generalisations in the plural

8 use the logical link word *but*

9 write some sentences for essays

10 collect information in a table by asking and answering questions

11 use some difficult expressions

12 try to guess what is coming next in a passage

You will be able to check your progress in the **Self-assessment** section at the end of the unit.

Preparing to read

A During a lecture on The Development of Money, you have made notes on the properties of silver and gold coins as money as follows:

> Properties of precious metal coins: attractive, durable, made of expensive material, internationally acceptable, generally recognisable as money, sought after as a commodity, available in medium units of value, heavy, yellow, expensive to insure, difficult to transport, difficult to forge, rare . . .

Pair or group work Discuss the properties of precious metal coins to make sure you understand them.

1 Can you add to the list?
2 Which of the properties are important for modern money?
3 Which properties would act as a hindrance to using money nowadays?

B Take one of the following types of money and check which of the above properties applies to it:

1 base metal coins (e.g. nickel, copper and alloy coins: pennies, 10p pieces etc.)
2 banknotes
3 bank accounts

C   Complete the table to show the difference between the *intrinsic* and *extrinsic* properties of money:

intrinsic (properties of the substance itself)	extrinsic (properties indirectly connected with the commodity)
1 gold non-corrosive, yellow, heavy,	rare, difficult to imitate, desirable as a thing of value,
2 base metal coins	
3 banknotes	
4 bank balances	

D   What do you know about the cost of money?

1 What raw materials are needed for **a** coins? **b** notes? **c** bank deposits?
2 What processes are used to produce the above types of money?
3 What kind of storage is needed for **a** gold? **b** banknotes? **c** bank deposits?
4 For what types of money are transport and insurance likely to be expensive?

The passage   *Bank money*

A   Read the passage twice quickly, so as to understand the gist of it.

B   Read it slowly, choosing the best of the alternative meanings on the left.

C   Answer the questions next to the passage.

Numbers in brackets refer to lines in the text.

1 What *properties* (1), for example? (Think of some intrinsic characteristics.)

2 What *functions* (2)?

3 *Less satisfactory* (4) than what?

4 When would *transport* (6) be necessary?

5 Where would *storage* (7) take place?

6 *absorb* (8) = soak up? waste? contain?

7 *resources* (8) = shocks? springs? wealth?

8 What sort of economies was the *banking system* (11) expected to make?

9 The *result* (15) of what?

consists . . . of (16) = is made up of

The intrinsic properties of the medium of exchange are not relevant in performing these functions; all that matters is that there should be a single agreed standard. But commodity moneys are less satisfactory as media of exchange
5   and stores of value. They suffer the drawbacks of costs of production in their creation, and costs of transport and storage of the money commodity. Exchange systems based on commodity moneys therefore absorb real resources which might otherwise have been directly applied to the
10   satisfaction of real wants.

The development of a banking system resulted from attempts to economise in the production and use of commodity moneys. This development was an evolutionary process, which will be examined in more detail in the next
15   chapter. Its result has been a monetary system where the money stock consists primarily of bank deposits, but with notes and coin playing an important supporting role.

10 *discharge* (21–2) = payment? firing? release?

11 Who needs to be confident?

'Representative money' such as bank notes can be distinguished from 'token money', such as bank deposits.
20 Bank notes, despite the promise to pay which they bear, are themselves legal tender which *must* be accepted in discharge of debts. Bank deposits are good only so long as there is confidence that they can easily be converted into legal tender money. Bank deposits are not legal tender for
25 a very simple reason. If they were, no bank would be under any legal obligation to repay depositors. For, since it is always permissible to discharge a debt by using legal tender, a bank could repay a depositor by simply crediting another account at the same bank.

Discussion

A   Write down the answers to the following questions: *marks*

1 From the point of view of the functions of money, the intrinsic properties of money are
a very important
b of no importance at all
c fairly important   (1)

2 Give an example of a 'single agreed standard' of your country.   (1)

3 Which type of money is unsatisfactory as a medium of exchange?   (1)

4 Which type of exchange system is cheaper? One based on
a gold
b banknotes
c bank deposits   (1)

5 What did the development of the banking system result from?   (1)

6 What part of the money supply is greater?
a bank deposits
b notes and coins   (2)

7 What is 'representative money'?   (1)

8 What is 'token money'?   (1)

9 *Legal tender* is money which must by law be accepted as payment. Why are bank deposits not legal tender?   (2)

Total (12)

B   Check your answers. Do you understand your mistakes, if any? Note your score.

Analysis

Vocabulary practice

Use a word or phrase from the text to replace the words in italics, altering the sentence where necessary.

1 The *characteristics* of bank deposits make them the form of money most suitable to modern economic requirements.   (paragraph 1)
2 Sometimes large sums of money are wasted on things which people do not really require; otherwise money can be spent on *the things there is a direct demand for*.   (paragraph 1)
3 The money *deposits together with the cash* in the country increase in times of inflation.   (paragraph 2)
4 They *changed* $3 million into sterling.
5 The bank *paid* the money *into* his account. (The bank . . . his account . . .)

What comes next?

A It is important to use your understanding of what you read to guess what is coming next in the text. From your reading of the passage, what will the next paragraph be about?
1 why most payments do not use legal tender
2 different ways of paying debts
3 various types of bank deposits
4 the importance of cash as legal tender

B Now read the fourth paragraph and the examination question which follows:

> 30   Having pointed out the difference between representative and token money, however, we must also note that this distinction is of very little practical significance to the individual holder of money. So long as there is general confidence in the ability of a bank to convert its deposit into
> 35   legal tender money, its deposits will be just as acceptable in settlement of debts as legal tender money. Indeed, the greater convenience and security of bank deposits may well make them more acceptable for a wide range of transactions.

Convenience and *security* (37) for whom?

What is meant by legal tender? With suitable examples explain why, in practice, business may prefer to receive debt payments in other ways. What dangers are there in accepting forms of payment other than legal tender? (*Associated Examining Board, GCE O Level, Commerce, November 1979*)

C Make a list of points you would use in answer to this question.

Find the main verb Supply the main verb from the passage for each underlined space:

Subject	Verb	
The intrinsic properties of the medium of exchange	are not	relevant in performing these functions:
all that matters	is	that there should be a single agreed standard.
But commodity moneys	1 _____	less satisfactory as media of exchange and stores of value.
They	2 _____	the drawbacks of costs of production in their creation, and costs of transport and storage of the money commodity.
Exchange systems based on commodity moneys therefore	3 _____	real resources which . . .
The development of a banking system	4 _____	attempts to economise in the production and use of commodity moneys.
This development	5 _____	
Its result	6 _____	
(lines 18–19)	7 _____	
. . .	8 _____	
. . .	9 _____	
. . .	10 _____	
If they were,	11 _____	

Generalisations

A Notice that generalisations (statements which are generally true) are usually expressed in the plural:

1 (page 10) Nowadays the use*s* of money *are* mostly economic.
2 (pages 19–20) Coin*s are* the best-known form of money. . . . Coin*s are* solid, attractive, hard-wearing and easy to handle.

Notice that the use of the plural form continues through longer generalisations.
3 (line 3) But commodity money*s are* less satisfactory as medi*a* of exchange and store*s* of value. They suffer the drawback*s* of cost*s* of production . . .

What is the singular form of *media*?

B Write down one word for each blank:

From the passage:
Exchange (1)_____ based on commodity (2)_____ therefore
(3)_____ up real (4)_____ which might otherwise have been directly applied to the satisfaction of real (5)_____ .

From the list of words below select one word for each blank and write it in the plural form:

payee cheque bank customer payment account

(6)_____ usually prefer (7)_____ to make (8)_____ using
(9)_____ because it is much cheaper and easier to debit drawers'
(10)_____ and credit the accounts of (11)_____ than it is to pay out and take in cash.

C Write down the *four* plural words in the generalisations in the second paragraph of the passage (p. 28).

Understanding 'but'   **A**   Look at these examples:

1 (p. 10) Any object that is used as money may be called *commodity money*.	But in order to understand the money object more clearly, we should ask, 'What was it used for?'
2 There are four economic functions . . .	But in the past the use of money was not limited to these . . .
3 Perhaps they (the various forms of money) combined some of these qualities.	But one thing is certain.
4 (p. 28) . . . all that matters is that there should be a single agreed standard.	But commodity moneys are less satisfactory as media of exchange . . .
5 Its result has been a monetary system where the money stock consists primarily of bank deposits,	but with notes and coin playing an important supporting role.

The word *but* is a logical connector used when you wish to compare or contrast ideas.

B   Look at the table below.

1   What is the logical relationship of the ideas on the right to those on the left? Is it a relationship of

addition?   Are the ideas on the right *added* to the ideas on the left?

condition?   Are the ideas on the right a *condition* of the ideas on the left being true?

contrast?   Are the ideas on the right *compared with* or *set against* the ideas on the left?

result?   Are the ideas on the right *results* of the ideas on the left?

2   For which relationships are the logical connectors *but* and *and* used?

C   Write six sentences from the table using *and* or *but*.

Money must have value for buying things	it needn't be valuable in itself
	it must be generally recognisable as money
Bank notes are legal tender	they must be accepted in settlement of debts
	large sums are usually paid by cheque
Coins are useful for operating machines	they can be used for public phone calls
	they are inconvenient to carry around

Test your reasoning

More difficult questions   Write down the answers:

1   Why are the intrinsic properties of the medium of exchange not relevant to the economic functions of money?
   a The economic functions operate regardless of the physical nature of money as long as it is generally acceptable.
   b Commodity moneys are expensive to produce and they absorb real economic resources.
   c The banking system could not have developed without becoming free of various forms of commodity money.

2 Why are commodity moneys unsatisfactory as a medium of exchange?

3 The second paragraph leads one to the conclusion that
   a Modern notes and coins are an important development of money.
   b Bank deposits are the most useful form of money.
   c The banking system developed as a result of attempts to economise in the production and use of commodity money.

4 Why are commodity moneys unsatisfactory as a store of value?

Sentence structures

A   All that matters is that . . . Study the structure of these sentences.

1 All that matters is that there should be a single agreed standard. (2–3)

2 The main thing is that there is an acceptable money object.

NOTE   1 and 2 are useful ways of concluding paragraphs.

3 Another point is that there must be a form of legal tender.

NOTE   3 is a good way of beginning a paragraph.

B   Use the information from the reading passages and the notes below to write sentences with the same structure as the examples above:

1 Another point . . . (must) . . . economies in the money system.

2 The only thing that counts . . . money in our account.

3 An important aspect of banking . . . economical forms of money.

4 It is essential . . . convenient coins for ordinary circulation.

5 It is crucial . . . (must) . . . complete confidence in the currency.

C   Without 'there is' and 'there are' Look at how the structure changes when you do not use *there* . . .

1 All that matters is that a single agreed standard should be generally accepted.

2 The main thing is that the money object is accepted as payment.

3 Another point is that every country must have legal tender.

D   Now make your own examples with the notes below, using *is/are*, *should be* or *must*:

1 The point to bear in mind . . . commodity moneys . . . expensive to produce.

2 Another factor . . . banking system . . . make economies in the money system.

3 It is vital . . . deposits . . . convertible into legal tender at short notice.

4 It is an advantage . . . bank deposits . . . very easily transferable.

E   Another useful sentence structure Study the structure of these sentences:

1 It is always permissible to discharge a debt by using legal tender. (26–27)

2 It is convenient to buy things in shops by using credit cards.

F   Now use the notes below to write similar sentences:

1 . . . economical . . . minimise cash in circulation . . . (persuade) the public to use cheques.

2 . . . easier . . . pay larger amounts . . . (write) cheques.

3 . . . safer . . . avoid carrying money around . . . (use) cheques.

4 . . . advisable . . . take good care of your bank card . . . (keep) . . . in a safe place.

5 . . . important . . . keep an eye on your expenditure . . . (complete) your cheque book counterfoils.

Extension

Ask and answer

A   Ask questions about the advantages and disadvantages of various forms of money, using the table below. Study the second table and fill it in as you receive answers to the questions:

What are the Are there any other	advantages of disadvantages of	gold coins bank notes bank deposits	as media of exchange as stores of value as measures of value	?

Part of the table is completed to help you.

	Media of exchange		Stores of value		Measures of value	
	Advantages	Disadvantages	Advantages	Disadvantages	Advantages	Disadvantages
gold coins						
bank notes						
bank deposits	**1** safe against loss **2** convenience **3** speed **4** distance no problem **5** cheap to move	**1** not legal tender so payment can be refused **2** possibility of forgery of cheques **3** not economical for small purchases e.g. bus tickets	**1** interest for deposits **2** security of deposits in banks **3** cheap to store	**1** current account deposits lose value in times of inflation	**1** any value from the smallest to the highest can be given a price **2** ease of circulation	nil

B Discuss your completed table with fellow students and make changes if necessary.

Self-assessment

A Answer the questions below without looking back at the previous pages:

marks

1 Are the extrinsic properties of commodity money important for modern economic purposes?   (1)

2 Give three extrinsic properties of modern bank notes.   (3)

3 Give three intrinsic properties of gold and silver coins.   (3)

4 Give three items in the costs of production of commodity money.   (3)

5 Which of the following is true, according to the passage?
The modern banking system was
a set up in the last few years
b set up in the twentieth century
c developed over a long period   (1)

6 What is legal tender?   (3)

7 Generalisations are usually expressed in the _____ .   (2)

8 What word is used to link contrasting meanings?
a but   **b** and   **c** then   (1)

9 Use the notes below to write good sentences:
a The fact . . . physical money . . . expensive . . . produce.   (3)
b . . . important point . . . economies can . . . (achieve) . . .
(use) bank money.   (4)
c It is a simple matter . . . increase the money supply . . .
(print) more banknotes.   (3)

Total (27)

B Check your answers in the Answer Key and correct your answers.
Do you understand the correct answer?
Make a note of your score out of 27; turn it into a percentage.

Unit 4 — Banking indexes and syllabuses

Preview

The aim in this unit is to practise ways of surveying the coverage (the C in SCOPE) of a passage or book before reading it. You will

1 compare a syllabus with the subject contents of a textbook

2 practise putting items in alphabetical order

3 find out some of the things one can learn from the arrangement of indexes

4 see how subject contents are organised

5 relate subjects to headings in a financial newspaper

There is also some practice of the following writing skills:

6 using or not using *the*

7 using capital letters

8 avoiding use of colloquial expressions

9 writing opening sentences

Practice

What does your book cover?

A Take one of your banking textbooks. Look at the Table of Contents and Introduction. Leaf through the pages. Examine the Index. Decide what the book sets out to teach.

B Write down, from the list below, *all* the subjects which you think your book deals with, including those which it *partly covers or touches on*.

Money
development of monetary
  economics
markets

Retail Banking
balance sheets – asset structure –
  liability structure
services
payment systems
distribution of cash
economic functions
control of (legislation)
operation and management

Wholesale Banking
company finance
flotations
finance of trade
consultancy
investment

Central Banking
government monetary policy
control of the banking system
government finance
government accounts

International Banking
monetary reform
development finance

Comparing lists of topics

A This activity will give you practice in scanning strategies to discover areas of common ground in two lists of topics. The aim is to discover what items of your *Practice and Law of Banking* syllabus are missing from the table of contents of the textbook *Teach Yourself Banking* by Valentine and Mason below.

First read through your syllabus and the table of contents as quickly as possible. Then do the exercises which follow as fast as you can, and compare your results with those of a friend.

Contents

personal loan accounts–revolving
credit schemes–budget accounts–
opening an account–closing an
account

policies–stocks and shares–Stock
Exchange securities–American-type
share warrants–Post Office issues–
National Savings Certificates–
building society shares and deposits–
unquoted stocks and shares–land
debentures–produce–Statute of
Limitations–right of 'set off'

B   Write down the major subject areas in your syllabus which are not covered in the textbook and which might be different in your country.

C   Which chapters of Valentine and Mason do you need to look at to find passages relevant to the items below? Give the numbers of *all* relevant chapters.

1 the role and rationale of financial intermediaries

2 money and finance

3 public finance

4 internal and external debt

5 the principles of taxation procedure and practice with regard to closing accounts by customers and by bankers

6 executors and trustees

7 the relationship of banker and customer

8 mandates and powers of attorney

9 the characteristics of negotiable instruments

10 forged endorsements

11 the role of capital in production

12 the public debt

D   Which of the above items would you expect to find in a Law of Banking textbook?

E   Which of the above items would you expect to find in an Economics textbook?

Alphabetical order

See how fast you can put words into alphabetical order. Study each of the examples below. Why do the words come in the order in which they appear? The order is that used by all dictionaries and indexes.
The words are taken from *A Dictionary of Banking* by F. E. Perry (Macdonald and Evans, 1979).

A   First letter order
example
  accept   **b**ank   **c**ash   **d**ebit   **e**xport   **f**orward exchange rate   **g**old

1 Put the following letters in alphabetical order. Do not take longer than one minute: THEBANKOFJURIL

2 Put the following items in alphabetical order:
debenture, equity, rights issue, blue chip, gilts, stock, goodwill, treasury bills

B   Second letter order
example
  d**a**mage   d**e**ad money   d**i**fference   d**o**llar   D**u**tch auction

1 Put the following words in alphabetical order:
royalty, risk, receiver, run, rate

2 Find in a dictionary and write down a sequence of five words ordered by their second letter.

C   Third letter order
example
  ca**l**l money   ca**n**cellation   ca**p**acity   ca**r**d index   ca**s**e law

1 Order the following expressions:
matrix, macro-economics, maximum load line, managed bonds, marked cheque

2 Find in a dictionary and write down a sequence of five words ordered by their third letter.

D   Fourth letter order

example

qualified acceptance   quantitative rebate   quarter days   quasi-money
quayage

1 Order the following expressions:
tenure, tenant, tenor, tendance, tenement

2 From a dictionary, write down a sequence of five words ordered
according to their fourth letters.

E   Fifth letter order

example

bill **b**rokers   bill **f**or collection   bill **i**n a set   bill **o**f entry

1 Put the following in the right order:
without reserve, withdrawal of a bill, with profits, withholding tax

2 Do the same again:
good for, good faith, goods, good consideration, goods and chattels

F   Order the following names of banks:
New Nigeria Bank, Bangkok Bank, Amsterdam–Rotterdam Bank,
State Bank of India, Deutsche Bank, Associated Japanese Bank,
Banco di Roma, Shanghai Commercial Bank, Development Bank of
Singapore, Banco do Brasil

Using indexes

A   Main heading or sub-heading?

Ensure that you can make full and effective use of the indexes of
textbooks. The word order rules used in dictionaries apply to indexes.
However, some items are subordinated to others. (These are indented.)
Look at this example:

Ideology, 167–8, 188–93
IMF, 135, 136
Income distribution, 51–3
Indian family planning, 60–62
Indian unemployment, 65
Industrial revolution,
  in Britain, 17–24
  in France, 25
  in Germany, 24–5
  in Japan, 27–8
  in the USA, 26–7
  in the USSR, 25–6
Industrialisation, 94–106
  and agriculture, 106, 116–18

1 How do you know which items are dealt with in more detail?
2 Which items are given only a passing reference in this book?
3 Guessing from this small section of the index, which of the following
statements would you agree with?
  a The author focuses mainly on political causes of the gap between
  rich and poor.
  b The author focuses mainly on historical reasons why there is such a
  large gap between rich and poor.
  c The author sees the International Monetary Fund as being mainly
  to blame for the poverty gap.

B   From this list, indicate which items are subordinate and should be indented:

cost control	costs
cost structure of business	allocated and proportioned
costing	classification of
information	direct and indirect
methods	fixed and variable
systems and techniques	labour
	marginal

C   One of the problems you will encounter when using indexes (if you have not done so already) is that of not finding the item you are looking for. Do you **a** give up looking in the book you are using? Or do you **b** think of some other heading under which the item you are looking for might come? It is wiser to do **b**.

Suggest other headings under which the following items could be looked up if they do not occur in the index of your banking textbook:

1 negotiable instrument
2 bank cards
3 overdrafts
4 agricultural credit
5 direct debit

Title and sub-titles

A   Study the list of headings taken from the Contents page of a book by John White, of the Overseas Development Institute. Now decide:
1 Which item is the title of the book?
2 Which item is the chapter heading?
3 Which items are chapter sections?
4 Which are subsections?

Try organising them in different ways, until you find one that works. The connecting lines give you some clues.

a   Subscriptions
b   Special funds
c   Evolution
d   Structure
e   Aims and functions
f   The African Development Bank   title
g   The Origins of the African Development Bank   chapter heading
h   Operations
i   Resources   chapter section
j   Organisation and management
k   Prospects   subsection
l   Membership, subscriptions and voting rights
m   The African Environment
n   Les demi-états ('the half states')
o   Regional Development Banks
p   The competition for projects
q   Staffing

B   Complete the diagram below from the list on the previous page:

1 title of book ⟶ ☐

2 chapter heading ⟶ ☐

3 chapter
sections

| ☐ | The Origins of the African Development Bank | Structure | Evolution | ☐ |

(section heading)

4 subsections

☐		Subscriptions
Aims and Functions		☐
Resources		Staffing
☐		☐
☐		Les demi-états

Check your answers in the Answer Key.

Newspaper indexes

The Financial Times   This is the front page index of the *Financial Times*.

American News ...	5	FT Actuaries	38	Racing	40	Others	41
Appointments:		Foreign Exchanges	29	Share Information	42, 43	Weather	44
UK	24	Gold Markets	28	Stock Markets:		World Trade News	6
International ...	31	Intl. Companies ...	30–33	London	39	**INTERIM STATEMENTS**	
Arts	20	Leader Page	22	Wall Street	34	Clive Discount	25
Base Rates	26	Letters	23	Bourses	34	Combined English	25
Commodities	28	Lex	44	Technology	14	**ANNUAL STATEMENTS**	
Companies UK ...	25–27	London Options ...	26	TV and Radio	40	Fleming Jap. Inv.	27
Crossword	20	Management	19	UK News:		Rotaprint	26
Entertain. Guide ...	20	Men and Matters	22	General	7, 8	**PROSPECTUS**	
European News ...	2, 3	Mining	26	Labour	10	$9\frac{1}{2}$% Treas. Stock	9
Euromarkets	30	Money Markets ...	29	Unit Trusts:			
Euro Options	26	Overseas News ...	4	Authorised	40		

For latest Share Index phone 01-246 8026

A   On which pages would you expect to find the news items below?
1 Zimbabwe cuts foreign currency allowances
2 Japan loan for Peru
3 West-Midland Co-operatives plan merger
4 Telecom's low cost acoustic couplers
5 Jamaica tries to woo South East Asian investors
6 France offers Russia grain
7 Dollar falls but pound strong
8 Early profit-taking on Wall Street
9 The British Fashion awards for 1982
10 Australian harvest down sharply
11 Pressure increases on banks to cut rates
12 Commonwealth and African loans

13 The Pound spot and forward
14 Helene of London lifts profits by 25%
15 Uranium production ceases at Mary Kathleen
16 Combined English Stores in loss after 28 weeks

B   Under which heading would you expect to find the following?
1 Malaysian rubber prices
2 The latest rate for the Swiss franc
3 Information about the offer for sale of a new government stock
4 Information about trades unions in Britain
5 An article about a new computer
6 Information about interest charges by your bank for a loan you have from it
7 News items about Australia
8 A section about an earthquake in Italy
9 Share prices in New York
10 Advertisements for jobs in various countries

Analysis

'the' again

'There should be a position in the bank for you, Miss Jones. Let's go talk with the manager.'

A   *the* is used to refer to something specific:
– the origins of banks
– the central bank (if you are discussing a particular country)
– the central banks (a specific collection of central banks)
– the Hong Kong & Shanghai Bank
– the fool who signed this cheque
– the beautiful girl who works in the bank opposite
– the remittance of funds by demand drafts
– the manager of the bank in the airport reception area
– the Finance Act
– the *Financial Times*

Notice also that *the* is required before abbreviations:
– the ECGD (the Export Credits Guarantee Department)
– the IBRD (the International Bank for Reconstruction and Development)
– the IMF (the International Monetary Fund)

B   You should not use *the* when you are generalising:
– Women should be encouraged to become bank managers . . .
– Bills of Exchange are credit instruments . . .
– Hong Kong banks are facing a crisis . . .
– Girls who work in banks are . . .
– Computer crime is increasing.

or when the expression is used in a general uncountable sense:
– Monetary policy has been a disaster.
– Security clearance was granted without hesitation.

or when the accepted expression does not use *the*:
– Cash in advance is required for this order.
– We usually pay by Letter of Credit.
– We were guaranteed credit.

C   Notice that in places where you have the option to use *the*, your decision affects your meaning:
– She gave him money. (She was kind to him.)
– She gave him the money. (i.e. a specific lot of money mentioned earlier)
– Your bank will give you advice. (i.e. general financial advice)
– Your bank will give you the advice. (i.e. the advice you need for this particular project)

D   Practice   Rewrite the following sentences, inserting *the* where necessary. (The number of *the*s you will need is shown in brackets.)
1 Third World countries are now paying back more money to banks than banks are lending them, according to president of World Bank.(4)
2 Speaking to European Management Forum, he said there was a net drain of $21 billion to rest of world.(3)
3 Outflow of funds from Third World, mainly caused by repayments of high interest loans, is much higher than recent estimates made by commercial banks.(3)
4 Transfer refers to new lending minus debt service payments on medium and long-term lending from private sector.(2)
5 Figures must be set against ones published earlier this week by Bank for International Settlements.(3)

Capital letters

Rewrite the following sentences, changing letters into capitals at the beginnings of names, titles and sentences:
1 mr clausen warned that it would take years to repair the damage done to third world prospects by the worst recession in forty years.
2 the bank's affiliate, the international development association, had just agreed a $9 billion funding.
3 the international monetary fund expects this april's meeting of its policy-making interim committee to go ahead.
4 although the us treasury, mr donald regan, said on wednesday he was quite willing to attend the meeting, which has been on the calendar since september, us officials are cool to the idea.
5 they believe the occasion will be used by france and some developing countries to push for a new allocation of special drawing rights, the imf currency.

Formality

The italicised words are too colloquial and are unacceptable for essays. Rewrite the sentences in a more formal style:
1 The *B of E* has been banker to the government for *ages*.
2 The government *ditched* the project when they *got wise to* the *crooks* who had *cooked it up*.
3 The manager decided to *ok* the loan after a *chat* with the customer who *filled him in on* the details of the project.
4 The exporter should ask his bank to send the documents *etc plus* the Bill of Exchange to the customer *via* his bank.
5 Several economic co-operation groups, *e.g.* the EEC, ASEAN and LAFTA, aimed to *drop* all import duties on each other's goods.

Sentences from headlines

A   Use the newspaper headings and the notes below to write realistic opening sentences for the news items:

examples   JAPAN LOAN FOR PERU   (agree/ provide)
Japan has agreed to provide a loan for Peru.

TELECOM'S FIRST ACOUSTIC COUPLER   (next week/ launch/ market)
British Telecom will launch its first low-cost acoustic coupler onto the market next week.

1 DOLLAR WEAK BUT POUND STRONG
   (last night/ remain/ European centres)
2 AUSTRALIAN HARVEST DOWN SHARPLY
   (this year/ was/ compared to last year)
3 GOVERNMENT ENQUIRY INTO BANK MERGER
   (just/ start/ between Barklouds and Bigloans banks)
4 PRESSURE ON BANKS TO CUT RATES
   (this week/ increase/ New York and London)
5 URANIUM PRODUCTION AT MARY KATHLEEN
   (following exhaustion of deposits/ end/ South Australia)

B   Now write opening sentences, providing additional details of your own:
1 COMMONWEALTH AND AFRICAN LOANS
2 INDIAN INSTRUMENTS GROUP FORMED
3 LUNDOP CAN SURVIVE SAYS NEW CHAIRMAN
4 BANK STRONGROOM CLEANED OUT

Self-assessment

A   Answer the questions below without looking at the previous pages:

marks

1 What does the C stand for in SCOPE?   (1)

2 Put the following in alphabetical order: drawer, drawn, draft, drachma, draw down   (3)

3 Explain one way you can tell how important an index item is by looking at the index of a book.   (2)

4 Give at least two things you can do if you can't find the item you are looking for in an index or list of contents.   (4)

5 *the* is used to refer to something   **a** general   **b** specific   **c** uncountable   (1)

6 Rewrite the following, inserting *the* where necessary. Also use capital letters where necessary:

soviet union officials cannot disclose exact figures for grain harvest over past two years, because they are still counting, said mr pyotr paska, deputy planning minister.   (8)

7 Rewrite the following in more formal English:

High interest rates are bad news for businesses because they have to fork out an awful lot of money to the banks for loans.   (6)

Total (25)

B   Now check your answers in the Answer Key. Do you understand your mistakes?

Unit 5   What is a bank?

Preview

In this unit you will learn about

1 basic principles of banking and bank lending

2 textual function – how sentences in a passage relate to each other logically

You will also practise

3 surveying the subject, coverage, organisation and purpose of the text before reading

4 looking again at logical link words and understanding how they work

5 writing sentences which explain the work of parts of the banking system

6 understanding uses of *can*, *could* and *might* to suggest possibility

7 tabulating notes

8 using vocabulary accurately

9 using connecting words to write about principles of bank lending, and

10 requesting and dealing with a request for a loan.

Preparing to read

Surveying before reading

A   Survey the subject of the passage 'What is a bank?' Ask and answer questions to determine how much you and your colleagues know about banks. Make notes of essential points.

1 What does a bank do? (make a list of activities)
2 What sort of bank is the nearest bank to you in your country? (clearing? savings? government? agricultural?)
3 Does it have branches? If so, how widespread are they?
4 What is your local bank like? (the people who work there? the customers? the building?)

5 What do you use the bank for? (savings account? current account? borrowing money?)

6 If you don't use it, why not?

7 Have you thought of other possible uses for your local bank?

B   The coverage Read the first and last paragraphs of the passage. What aspect of a bank's work does the passage cover?

1 its economic functions?
2 its customer services?
3 work in a branch?
4 loans to customers?
5 bank architecture?
6 the structure of banks?

C   The organisation Like other texts, the passage 'What is a bank? has a structure. It is organised in a certain way. Look at the list of possible subject headings below. As you read the text, see how they contribute to its structure.

bank functions: borrowing, lending, supplying cash . . .
customer services: taking deposits, operating accounts, changing
                    money . . .
economic functions: distributing money to different parts of the country,
                    creating money, keeping reserves . . .

D   The writer's purpose Which of the following things do you think the writer is trying to do?

1 give instructions on how to use a bank?
2 define a bank for someone who has never heard of the idea?
3 describe the work of a branch bank?
4 show how a bank is part of the economic system?

If you can get a clear idea of what the writer is doing by glancing through parts of the text before reading, it will help you to read it faster and understand it better.

The passage   *What is a bank?*

A   Read the passage through quickly so as to understand the gist of it.

B   Then read it through more slowly so as to understand the detail.

C   Now go through it again, answering the questions on the left.

Numbers in brackets refer to lines in the text.

1 The inverted commas show that this statement is: (a) true (b) false (c) doubtful

2 Find an expression above equivalent to *cash* (4).

3 Which word above foreshadows *left luggage office* (3)?

We usually answer this question by saying, 'It's a place where you leave money.' This is the first idea that comes into our heads. We see a bank as a sort of left luggage office for spare cash, which we can withdraw from time to time.

5   However, some people do not deposit their money in banks. There was once an employee of the Thai Farmers'

4 Which word above does *job* (7) refer back to?

5 Why would they have to *dig* (8)?

6 Which *bank* (11)?

7 *Deposit* (12) of what?

8 The *door* (13) of what?

9 *Interest* (16) on what?

10 What *proceeds* (17)?

11 *At a higher rate* (17) of what?

12 *Borrowing* (18) what?

13 What words show that this paragraph is taking up the title question again?

14 Find a synonym (25) for *excess* (22).

15 List five words which go together in a set.

16 Find two words (24) which are synonymous with *makes it available* (26).

17 *Lent* (29) what?

18 *The North* (29) of what?

19 What was the first function of banks mentioned?

20 Find a verb (24–27) which foreshadows *liquid*.

21 What is an important part of a bank's liquid reserves (34)?

22 *This proportion* (36) of what?

23 In what way does cash *evaporate* (41) if you just keep it in storage?

24 *Enough* (47) what?

25 What *reservoir* (48)?

26 *Sufficient* (48–9) what?

Bank who dealt with such people. It was his job to go round the villages persuading farmers to dig up their secret hoards of cash and deposit them in the bank. He usually

10 had to give them a few drinks before they would tell him where they had buried their money. But once the bank had got hold of it, it did not simply put each deposit in a safe with the owner's name on the door. This would have been very uneconomical and it would have been better to leave

15 the money in the ground. The bank could far more profitably pay the farmers interest–as an incentive to deposit their savings–and lend out the proceeds at a higher rate to businesses or other farmers. By borrowing and lending in this way, a bank makes a profit.

20 So banks are not just left luggage offices for cash. They are also like a combined drainage, storage, irrigation and water supply system. Ideally, the system drains excess water from wet land, stores it in tanks or reservoirs and distributes it to farmers and households. In the same way,

25 an effective banking system mops up surplus wealth in some areas and makes it available in other areas where it is needed. The English banks of the eighteenth century were doing this when they borrowed from the farmers in East Anglia and lent to the new factory builders of the North.

30 The function of the banks was to mobilise the liquid resources of the country.

A banking system, however, differs from a drainage and irrigation system in one important respect. If it is efficient, it has no large liquid reserves. In Britain cash is a mere 8b

35 of all the banks' total assets. For the banks have learnt through long experience that this proportion is enough to pay all those people who want to draw cash out for daily use. Some of this cash, however, (4%) is kept as a permanent reserve in the vaults of the central bank. This is like

40 the water in a reservoir which is doing nothing. As long as it is in storage it is useless. Also it is evaporating and the reservoir has to be maintained, so it costs money to keep it there. In the same way, cash in the banks is uneconomical for, like gold, it earns no interest, and it is expensive to

45 keep and handle. So an important function of the banks is to keep the amount of cash in the system to a minimum. But there must always be enough in the tills of each branch bank for withdrawals. The reservoir must always have sufficient to supply farmers, factories and households.

What does the passage say?

A   Write short answers to the following as quickly as possible.

marks

1 What is the first idea of a bank that we think of when asked 'What is a bank?'   (1)

2 Which of these statements agrees with the first paragraph:
a A bank is a depository for cash.
b People usually regard banks as depositories for cash.
c The writer regards banks as depositories for cash.   (1)

3 How did the official of the Thai Farmers' Bank find out from some farmers where they had hidden their money?   (2)

4 How did the Thai Farmers' Bank persuade farmers to deposit money in the bank?   (2)

5 What did the bank do with the farmers' money?   (2)

6 What four agricultural and domestic services are the activities of banks compared with?   (4)

7 How does the writer summarise the four activities of banks?   (4)

8 Why is it uneconomical for banks to hold a lot of cash?   (3)

Total (19)

B   Now check your answers with the key. How much did you score? Keep a record of your score and percentage mark.

Analysis

Logical link words

A   **Types of explanation** Find the logical link words listed below (1–6) in the passage. How do they connect up with the sentences which come before them? Decide which of the logical operations (a–e) each link word performs.
The numbers in brackets refer to line numbers.

logical link words	logical operation
1 However (5, 32, 38)	a reason
2 But (11, 47)	b condition
3 and (14, 17, 29)	c contrast
4 So (20, 42, 45)	d consequence
5 If (33)	e addition
6 For (35, 44)	

This does not mean that the other sentences in the text have no logical connection with one another. They do. But you have to discover the connection from the sense.

B   Study the way the sentences listed below work in the passage and decide which of the logical operations on the right they perform:

sentences	logical operation
1 We usually answer . . . (1)	**a** comparison
2 The English banks . . . (27)	**b** narration
3 The function . . . (30)	**c** response
4 This is like . . . (39)	**d** justification
5 There was once . . . (6)	**e** exemplification
6 This would have been . . . (13)	**f** summary

C   Notice the following points:

1 *There was once an employee . . .*, as well as functioning as narration, is also a sign-post phrase. It points out the beginning of a new section in the text: a story.

2 Many of the functions overlap with each other. A sentence may function as an illustration at the same time as offering comparison or exemplification.

3 Nearly all the sentences function as explanation, so it is not clear to describe any one sentence as 'explanation' only.

Writing sentences

A   **It was his job to . . .** Study the form of these examples:

1   . . . employee . . . job . . . villages persuade . . . farmers to deposit secret hoards of cash in the bank. (go round)

It was the employee's job to go round the villages persuading farmers to deposit their secret hoards of cash in the bank. (line 7)

2   . . . the small branch manager . . . function . . . all the departments . . .

It is the small branch manager's function to supervise all the departments, making sure that they are doing their work properly.

This sort of sentence is very useful when you are writing about functions and job descriptions.

B   Use the notes to help you write similar sentences:

1   . . . cashier . . . job . . . customer's money keep . . . a record of all transactions (pay out and receive)

2   . . . banking system . . . function . . . funds in areas of surplus make . . . them available in areas of . . . (absorb)

3   . . . accountant . . . responsibility . . . customers at the counter make . . . sure that any problems are solved correctly (meet)

4   . . . security clerk . . . concern . . . securities received by the manager from customers ensure . . . they cover the bank's advances (examine)

5   . . . statement . . . function . . . all transactions enable . . . customers to monitor their accounts (display)

Continue writing similar sentences using the notes below:

6 foreign clerk/ help customers about to go abroad/ provide them with travellers' cheques and foreign currency

7 remittance clerk/ sort out cheques and credits paid in by customers/ divide them up according to the banks they are drawn on

8 money market/ stabilise exchange rates/ provide a place where demand and supply can meet

9 clearing system/ account for all receipts and payments in the country/ total all credits and debits between the banks

10 central bank/ advise the government/ execute its monetary policy

C   Look at the following sentence:

By borrowing and lending in this way, a bank makes a profit (ll. 18–19)

Write similar sentences using the notes below:

1 . . . raise . . . interest rates, the government . . . control the money supply   (try)

2 . . . make . . . easy loans available, the World Bank . . . development (encourage)

3 . . . borrow . . . from a merchant bank, the company . . . specialised advice   (obtain)

4 . . . provide . . . financial support to agriculture, they . . . make the country self-sufficient in food   (hope to)

5 . . . keep . . . the amount of cash to a minimum, the banking system . . . big economies   (achieve)

D   Suggesting possibility   How is possibility suggested by these sentences?

1 The bank could far more profitably pay the farmers' interest and lend out the proceeds at a higher rate to businesses or other farmers. (ll. 15–18)

2 A bank could repay a depositor by simply crediting another account at the same bank. (p. 29, ll. 27–9)

Which of the above examples refers to the possibility in the past? Which one refers to unlikely possibility in the present? Here is another example (p. 20, ll. 23–6):

3 For shopping, small coins of base metals can be used.

4 Coins of larger denominations can be made of silver and gold.

E   Discussion   What sort of possibility do the above examples express? Think of other examples using *might*.

Extension

Tabulating notes

A   Study the three diagrams below, which demonstrate three ways of tabulating notes on the passage. Then answer the questions that follow:

Diagram 1

What is a bank?	
Paragraph 1	a place to keep money
2	profits from borrowing and lending
3	mobilising liquid resources
4	supplying finance to borrowers
5	keeping cash in the system to a minimum

Diagram 2

What is a bank?	
Customer services	Economic functions
Taking deposits and paying interest	Absorbing financial surpluses

Diagram 3

What is a bank?	
Borrowing	Lending
Distribution of cash	Reserves

1 Which table, in your opinion, shows most clearly how the writer has organised the content of the passage?
2 Which frame helps you with your banking studies best?
3 Which frame represents your own interests, if these are different from your banking studies?

Compare your conclusions with the analysis of the tables given in the Answer Key.

B   Draw one of the organisation frames, or design one of your own, large enough so that you can make notes on the passage. Then fill in the frame with notes.

Accurate use of words

Choose the best expression to complete each sentence:

1 Clearing banks have to retain sufficient (cash/reserves/assets) to meet (repayments/deposits/withdrawals).
2 Interest is the (proceeds/incentive/profit) offered by banks to persuade people to (deposit/entrust/invest) their (hoards/liquid resources/surplus wealth) with them.
3 The World Bank tries to ensure that its loans are used (effectively/efficiently/appropriately) to bring about economic development.

4 An (efficient/effective/economical) banking system maintains full
banking services while keeping costs to a minimum.
5 An (effective/economical/efficient) banking system maintains all the
banking services required by its customers.
6 Banks are required to place some of their (surplus wealth/liquid
resources/reserves) with the Central Bank.

Further practice with words

A   Write down the missing words from the following paragraphs. Each
word relates back in some way to something that has gone before. Clues
to that relationship are given in the notes on the left:

Notes

1/2 refers to second part of title
 3 relates to *money*
 4 consequence
 5 person the bank lends to
 6 opposite of 5
 7 contrast
 8 noun form of adjective in
    previous line
 9 addition
10 refers to *the borrower*
11 condition
12 refers to *a customer*
13 a definite *manager*
14 refers to *manager*
15 known facts
16 condition
17 refers to *business concern*
18 opposite of *business concern*
19 addition
20 opposite of *income*
21 contrast
22 same as 15

Bank lending
What does a bank need to know?

In answering (1)_____ (2)_____ one must remember that banks
lend money (3)_____ has been lent to them by their depositors.
(4)_____ a banker has a special duty to ensure that the (5)_____
will be able to repay. Like other (6)_____ , a bank will only want
5 to lend to customers whom it considers to be honest and reliable.
(7)_____ (8)_____ is not enough. A bank will (9)_____ want
to be satisfied that the borrower is able to carry out (10)_____
proposals.
    (11)_____ a customer wishes to borrow, (12)_____ first step is
10 to discuss (12)_____ proposals with (12)_____ bank manager.
What will (13)_____ manager want to know? (14)_____ will
probably already have a great deal of helpful (15)_____ about the
customer and his affairs. (16)_____ the customer is a business
concern, the manager will know what (17)_____ makes or trades
15 in, the size of the business, the success (17)_____ has achieved
and its financial position. In his ordinary dealings with (18)_____
(18)_____ , the banker will know their occupations, (19)_____
will probably have some idea of their income and (20)_____ – and
of their liabilities and commitments. (21)_____ , when a customer
20 comes to borrow, the manager will need to add a considerable
amount of detail to this background (22)_____ .

B   Use the notes below to continue writing on the subject 'Bank
lending: What does a bank need to know?' Begin each paragraph with
the sentences provided.

Paragraph 3   The customer will naturally want to explain . . .
(the purpose of the loan, the way the money is to be used, request by a
personal customer contrasted with that of a business concern,
simple/complicated, the need for assessment)

Paragraph 4   Closely related to the purpose of the loan is the amount.
The manager will want to be sure that . . .
(ability of the customer to repay, business concern . . . accountant's
figures, the need to minimise the risks, ensure the amount borrowed is
sufficient to carry out the business proposals . . .)

Paragraph 5   The manager will then ask the customer to tell him how
he plans to repay the . . . and for how long he needs to . . .
(banks' preference for short term loans, the need to tailor loans to suit
different requirements, cover particular items of expenditure, repayment
within agreed time limits)

Negotiation simulation

A   The case for a loan Half the class prepare the customer's case and the other half the bank manager's. Then simulate meetings in pairs of a customer with a bank manager.

The customer's case

1 You are a customer of your local bank, urgently requesting a loan from the manager. It is absolutely vital that you obtain this loan and you must prepare a careful request knowing that the manager is likely to refuse.
2 Take into account the points covered in the writing. You can use your imagination to create your own facts for a business project or to make a purchase.
3 Make notes covering all the points the manager is likely to ask you about. Prepare your notes in such a way as to leave space for possible points of enquiry on the part of the manager.

NOTE   Your three written paragraphs cover only some of the aspects of the loan situation. What other points would your bank manager want to raise?

The bank manager's case

1 You are the manager of the local branch of a large bank and you have an appointment with an old customer who is going to ask you for a loan or overdraft.
2 You have received instructions from your head office that only the most important requests for finance should be granted but it has been left to your judgement to decide what is important.
3 In the interview, go into all aspects of the request thoroughly and try to pick holes in the customer's case.
4 The interview should be prepared with notes on the customer's past record. You will need to ask the customer about this. But you can provide some information about the customer from your own records.

NOTE   Your three written paragraphs cover only some aspects of the loan situation. What other points would you want to raise with your customer?

B   Imagine yourself in the situation shown in the cartoons below.
1 Can you argue a case with the bank manager? (Perhaps the man's wife has removed some of the furniture or the central heating boiler.)
2 If you were the bank clerk, what advice would you give the man?

"I'M AFRAID GETTING A DIVORCE DOESN'T COME UNDER A HOME-IMPROVEMENT LOAN."

"OUR LOAN OFFICERS ARE CONSIDERING YOUR APPLICATION NOW, SIR."

Self-assessment

A   Answer the questions below without looking back at the previous pages:

marks

1 True or false:
   a All sentences in a text are connected to previous sentences by logical link words.
   b Every sentence in a text has some logical connection with what goes before.
   c You can rely on understanding how each sentence is related to what goes before it only by the sense.   (3)

2 Write single sentences (like in **Writing sentences, A**) describing the purpose and the work of each of the following:
   a a bank manager
   b a night security guard
   c a central bank (Start your sentence: 'One of the functions of a central bank is to . . .')   (15)

3 Write two sentences describing what it is possible for you to do with money using bank services.   (10)

4 Complete the following with one word for each space:
   a The central bank keeps the country's foreign exchange
   _____.   (3)
   b Cashless methods of making payments using bank cards would make the banking system more _____ though they may not be very popular.   (3)

5 Complete the following:
   a Banks make a profit by . . .   (3)
   b A major function of banks in the economy is to mobilise
   . . .   (3)

Total (40)

B   Check your answers in the Answer Key or seek the help of an instructor. Make sure you understand your mistakes.

Banking problems: Question analysis and the reader's purpose

"IF THE DOLLAR IS FLOATING, WHY IS MY BANK ACCOUNT SINKING?"

Preview

This unit is about analysing essay questions and reading tasks. The aim is to make your studies more cost-effective in terms of the energy and time you put into them.

A All questions can be analysed into two components and two sub-components:

1 The topic or topics which answer the question, 'What is this question about?'
   a things which are common knowledge (given information)
   b things that the question introduces (requested information)

2 The function or operational task which answers the question, 'What does this question want me to do?'
   a the general or overall function of your essay
   b detailed functions of the different parts of your essay

B Just as you need to analyse a problem before you solve it, you need to analyse an essay question before writing an answer to it. So the first part of this unit can be represented by the following diagram:

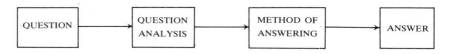

A similar diagram shows what the second part of this unit is about:

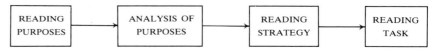

Preparing to answer questions

Topic analysis

A Match the questions with the topics.

Questions

1 Do you buy foreign currency?
2 Do you open Saturday mornings?
3 Have you received a draft from my bank?
4 Why can't you cash my cheque?
5 Can you please tell me the balance of my account?

Topics

a the state of an account
b the arrival of a draft
c the bank's policy on buying currency
d the customer's cheque
e the bank's hours of business

B   The topics of the above question–answer situations are obvious. Now look at how the topics shift with a shift of the question. The questions and topics are already matched:

Questions	Topics
1 To what extent are banks prepared to buy foreign currencies?	foreign currency margins and handling costs
2 Should banks open on Saturday mornings?	bank opening hours and union negotiations
3 Which is the best way to remit funds from one country to another?	methods of sending funds internationally
4 What are the reasons why a bank might not cash a cheque?	faulty and forged cheques
5 Account for recent changes in banks' sending out statements.	economies in bank administration costs

Question functions   This refers to the operational task of the *answer*. What is the questioner actually asking you to do?

A   Consider these two questions written by readers of *Your Business* magazine on the subject of bank references:

1 Why do banks insist on references when opening accounts?

2 I have just been refused a hire-purchase facility because my banker's reference was not good enough. Can I find out what the bank said?

The function of the editor is to give advice to both these readers. But 'giving advice' is too general a level of analysis, because it doesn't go deep enough to tell you anything. Now read the editor's answers and decide what other functions he carries out besides the overall function of giving advice:

1   *Why do banks insist on references when opening accounts?*

    Many in fact now only ask you to identify yourself, for example by driving licence or security pass.

    References used to be required so that
5 banks could obtain protection from a customer's fraudulent activities under the Cheques Act 1957, but with so many accounts being opened now, many regard them as unnecessary formality which only delays matters.
10 Building societies do not require references, and the banks are trying to compete with them.

2   *I have just been refused a hire-purchase facility because my banker's reference was not good enough. Can I find out what the bank said?*

    You can always ask the bank or the hire purchase company to let you know exactly what was said in the reply, but neither party is obliged to tell you anything. Banks never give
5 bad replies. They always base their reply on the information in their files and try to be as helpful as possible. However, it is not so much what they say, but more what they don't say and users of these references are becoming
10 very skilled in interpretation. Next time you think someone will enquire about you from your bank, it may not be a bad idea to speak to the bank and put them fully in the picture.

In answer to question 1 the editor gives information. He gives a short summary of the situation regarding references for opening accounts as it stands in the UK (1984).

In answer to the second question, the editor
– gives information (*Banks never give bad replies.*)
– makes a suggestion (*Next time . . .*)

B   The commonest functions required in essay questions are:
1 discuss
2 describe
3 explain

These are used by examiners in a very general way but you need to analyse questions further. Look at some of the other essay writing functions below. Numbers 4–12 have been matched with the kind of expressions you might use:

4 clarify	Another way of putting it is . . .
5 exemplify	For instance . . . This can be seen in . . .
6 enumerate	Firstly there is . . . Then . . . Finally . . .
7 suggest	A new branch could be opened . . .
8 evaluate	The plan was a moderate success. Yet it must be said . . .
9 plan	In the first part of this essay we shall look at . . .
10 contrast	However . . . But . . . On the other hand . . .
11 define	Fraud is when . . . A bounced cheque is . . .
12 summarise	To put it briefly . . . In short, managers should . . .

Now match the remaining functions with suitable expressions:

13 identify	**a** Another way of putting it is . . .
14 announce	**b** Using cheques is far safer than carrying cash.
15 compare	**c** Cheque books are normally issued with the name of . . .
16 hypothesise	**d** Such a scheme would be completely unworkable.
17 inform	**e** It is certainly true that the cheque was false, but . . .
18 report	**f** Cheque books will be available in two colours.
19 conclude	**g** The first example is a cheque, the second is a Bill.
20 reject	**h** Cheques were invented in . . .
21 concede	**i** Cheques were probably invented in . . .
22 analyse	**j** So it is clear that . . . Cheques should therefore be . . .
23 restate the problem	**k** The work of the branch can be divided into five main sections, each of which has two subdivisions.

NOTE   1 The above are examples of ways the functions on the left can be expressed. They can be written in other ways as well.
2 The functions listed are common examples, not a complete list.

C   As we have seen above, accuracy in identifying the question task is essential if you are to write a good answer. It's of little value to say the question wants you to *describe* developments, because this function is too vague and general. It could be applied to anything:
– Describe the main services . . . (*Enumerate*)
– Describe the work of the central bank . . . (*Analyse*)
– Describe the current exchange control regulations in . . . (*Summarise*)
In each case the word in brackets identifies the task more accurately. It tells you clearly what you are to do.

D Practice Decide on three question functions that could be used to answer each question. Choose your functions from the list (1–23) in **B** above:

1 Trace the development of commercial banking in England and Wales from the London goldsmiths of the seventeenth century to the 'big four' London clearing banks of the 1980s.

2 Describe the main assets that appear in a commercial bank's balance sheet, indicating their special characteristics, and their relationships to banking business.

3 Why does a bank need liquidity? How does a bank provide for liquidity in the use it makes of the deposits entrusted to it?

4 The whole business of banking depends upon maintaining the confidence of depositors. What steps does a banker take to safeguard the depositors' interests?

5 A recent US presidential commission overwhelmingly rejected a return to the gold standard. What are the limitations and advantages of basing currency on gold?

6 'A bank can create its own deposits'. Trace briefly the steps by which this occurs.

Choosing the right reply

A Here are some more questions sent in by readers of *Your Business* magazine.
– Study the two examples. Read the question first and notice the topic title and function of the reply.
– Then read the answer. Decide whether the editor has accurately identified the question task in giving his reply.

Question	Reply
1 *I am thinking of trying to persuade my staff to be paid by cheque. Are any problems likely?* *Topic title:* Paying Employees by Cheque *Function of reply:* clarification of the problem	**a** If your staff have bank accounts, there should be no real problems but, if any do not, arrangements will need to be made for the cheques to be cashed, preferably at your bank. This will require specific authorisation by the directors who should insist on strict identification requirements. So you can ensure that the right person receives the money.
2 *Profitability and recent sales have resulted in a build up of cash in the bank account. What is the best way of investing it?* *Topic title:* Cash in the Bank *Function of reply:* to inform	**b** Cash should be treated like any other asset and made to work for you in making profits. For amounts over £10,000, you should ask your bank about money market accounts where deposits can be made from "overnight" to up to five years fixed depending on the customer's requirements. Under £10,000 there are other schemes apart from deposit accounts which could be suitable.

B Now you will decide the topic and the function.
– Read and discuss the questions only. Choose a title for each question.
– Decide the most appropriate function for each reply.
– Then decide which of the replies matches each question.
  Does the reply fulfil the function you decided upon?

(If you are working in a group, one of you should pose the question, choosing it at random; then another member of the group should give an appropriate answer. A third member should find the correct answer from the series of answers on the right-hand side of the page.)

3 *We are beginning to get established in international markets and wish to streamline our receipts and payments to avoid unnecessary exchange conversion costs.*

4 *I was upset recently when my bank telephoned because the borrowing on the company's account was above the limit agreed although I had paid in more than sufficient funds at another branch.*

5 *Our bank makes a charge for returning cheques with our statements. Does this practice vary from bank to bank?*

6 *Is it true that my cheque guarantee card is no longer valid abroad?*

7 *I have asked my bank if it will issue me with a cheque card on the company's account. It refused.*

8 *We want to set up local banking arrangements for our branch in the West country. What should we do?*

9 *Mine is basically a cash business and I am loathe to keep large sums of money either on the premises or at home overnight. How can this be avoided?*

c Banks always charge and credit interest based on the cleared balance rather than the balance appearing on your statement. The cleared balance is computer calculated and takes into consideration the time taken for the bank to receive payment for cheques credited to your account. For example, a credit containing a cheque for £100 paid in on a Monday morning will be credited to your account that day but the cheque will not reach the bank it is drawn on until the Wednesday—three working days. While your statement may show your account to be £100 less overdrawn, the interest calculation will not be reduced until the Wednesday, the day the cheque is paid and the balance becomes "cleared".

d Apart from investing in a safe of your own, you can approach your bank to see if they provide night safe facilities. The bank simply holds the money in a special safe overnight, then pays it into your account the following day. There is a charge of about £3.00 for each special wallet issued in which the money is put.

e Some banks are happy to provide such a service but others are very reluctant in view of the staff costs involved. While these banks may agree to continue the service for old customers, they will rarely agree to new requests.

f Since the abolition of exchange control it is possible for companies to maintain foreign currency accounts with their bank, which are especially useful when receiving and making payments in the same currency. These accounts work exactly the same way as an ordinary current account and cheque books and paying-in books are available.

g When dealing with a new supplier it is not always possible to establish the credit terms within the time allowed and for substantial orders, they will be unwilling to accept cheques and allow collection before they are cleared. In this case, it is best to use the telephone transfer system which enables guaranteed funds in excess of £10,000 to be

10 *I have a standing order on my account for £250 on the first day of each month. If there is not enough money in my account on the 1st, will the bank check to see if funds are paid in at a later date, and then make payment?*

11 *I have an urgent need for some materials from new suppliers. How can I get funds to them quickly?*

12 *My bank referred to my "cleared" balance when I queried interest charged on my account. What does it mean?*

transferred between banks on the same day. The charge for this service varies but will cost in the region of £15.

h A standing order is a specific instruction to pay money on a certain date. If there is not enough money, the bank may give you a temporary overdraft but this may cost as much as 19–20%, on an annual basis. The bank will not normally check on any other day of the month, so you will otherwise have to make your own arrangements for payment.

i The British banks have decided to withdraw from previous arrangements in Europe and now issue special "Eurocheques" and "Eurocheque cards". The amount of the guarantee is £75 and application should be made through some local bank.

j Most important are the security arrangements—who signs the cheques, who collects the money and the identification required—which should be clear from the start. A bank will usually cash a cheque only for an authorised representative of a company.

k As a matter of policy, agreed by all banks, cheque cards are not normally available on company accounts and indeed you would find them unacceptable in most outlets. The reason propounded is that a business should have established relationships with its suppliers and credit cards should fill any gap.

l It is very difficult for a particular branch to know precisely what is in the current clearing system and instead of making extensive and time consuming enquiries, it is easiest to contact the customer. How tactfully the bank manager behaves is another question.

C   Check that you have matched questions and replies correctly by referring to the Answer Key.

Analysis

Language

A   What sort of English should we use to express the functions listed in **B** on page 58? See how the editor of *Your Business* expressed himself in his replies:

What the writer was doing	Notes
Reply **a** *clarifying* If your staff . . . but if any do not . . . This will require . . .	The editor . . . establishes alternative possibilities
Reply **b** *informing* Cash should be treated . . . For amounts over £10,000, you should ask your bank . . . There are other schemes . . . which could be suitable	. . . makes a suggestion (in the last sentence)

Reply **c** *informing*
Banks always charge . . .
For example, . . .   (*exemplifying*)

Reply **d** *suggesting* and *informing*
Banks always charge . . .
The bank simply holds . . .

Reply **e** *informing*   Notice the sub-function
While these banks . . . they will rarely . . .   *qualifying*.

Reply **h** *defining*
A standing order is a specific . . .

Reply **j** *restating the problem*   – a good way to begin an
Most important are . . .   essay

Reply **l** *explaining*   Notice that *explaining* is done
                                                 when there is some unsolved
                                                 problem posed by the
                                                 question.

B   Use the same kind of language in your essays, matching the
expressions to your purpose. Here are some examples of how to write
for three of the functions listed in **B** on page 58:

1 *enumerate:*   The task of supervising the banks can be sub-divided as
   follows: Firstly the Bank . . . Then the authorities regulate the
   reserves . . . In addition . . . Fourthly . . . Finally . . .

2 *evaluate:*   The work of the central bank should be seen in terms of
   the aims of government policy and the degree of success the Bank has
   in carrying it out. In addition we can assess the effectiveness of the
   Bank's normal work supervising the banking sector.

3 *analyse:*   The work of the central bank is normally divided into two
   main areas. There is considerable overlap of functions but it is
   important to break down the Bank's work into its component parts.
   In this way one can study what the Bank does in detail.

C   Now read each of the following sets of expressions and decide which
of the functions listed below apply to them:

announcing, reporting, appreciating, conceding, reasoning, identifying,
summarising, comparing, hypothesising, planning

   1 The policy of high interest rates which has been pursued in the USA
   and other countries recently is disastrous. While one can understand
   the ideas underlying this monetarist approach to the economy, there
   are several arguments that can be advanced against it.

   2 The economist who originated this line of thinking was John
   Maynard Keynes.

   3 A possible explanation is that . . .
   Several interpretations can be advanced to explain this development,
   but the most plausible is . . .
   This can be attributed to . . .
   These may be due to . . .

4 The first part of this essay will deal with . . .
In the second half . . .
We will now go over the . . . then we will look into . . .

5 Certainly payment by documentary Bills is the least troublesome in terms of time and effort, but . . .
To a great extent this is true, but other factors cannot be ignored . . .

6 In 1979 the Banking Act was passed which formalised for the first time control of the banking system by the Bank of England.
In November one of the directors took out a personal loan.
A shareholders' meeting was held on June 18th.

7 From now on exchange control rules will be strictly enforced.
The bank will remain open for half an hour longer every afternoon.
A shareholders' meeting will be held on June 18th.

8 The most obvious difference between the US and the UK banking systems is . . .
Businesses are normally taxed at the end of the financial year while individuals have to pay as they earn.

9 The essentials of the situation are . . .
The main issue is simply one of . . .
To sum up, one can say that . . .
Essentially . . .
In short, the factors which dominate the situation are . . .

10 Such work is vital to the well-being of the community . . .
The chief advantages are . . .
Without such financial services, the business community would be severely handicapped.

Reading purposes

A   As well as analysing your essay writing tasks you also need to analyse your reasons for reading. The aim is to save time and energy and help you to read in the most effective way. Below is a list of possible reasons for reading. Go through the list and decide which ones best apply to you.

Reasons for reading

1 I am a student and all students have to read.

2 I need *more information* about OPEC countries' balance of payments and I know it comes somewhere in this book.

3 I need to have *another view or opinion* about monetary policy.

4 I want to improve my *background knowledge* of the gold standard.

5 I am new to the subject of branch management and I want a good *introductory book* which isn't too technical.

6 I like reading and want something I can *relax* with.

7 I want to *know how* the cash dispensing system *works*.

8 I am *not sure whether I really need to read* this book or not.

9 I am *interested* in banking, apart from my exam aims, and would like to know more about the historic role of banks and colonial empires.

10 I need to *bring myself up-to-date* on the world debt crisis.

11 I want something really *exciting* to read while travelling.

12 I need to find *something easier to understand* than the book I have been recommended.

13 I *need some facts* to put in an essay.

14 I am a professional and I have to *keep abreast of all developments* in banking.

15 I want to *check that I haven't missed any important points* in an essay I am preparing to write.

16 I *like the sound of words and images of language.*

17 I want to *improve my knowledge and use of English.*

18 A customer of our bank wants to borrow money for her business and I *need to be acquainted with the technical aspects* of it.

19 I have to *research the contribution* of agricultural credit to development in three countries.

20 I am *interested in political developments* and how they affect the future of banking services in my country.

21 I want to *broaden my experience of the great literature of* the nineteenth century.

22 I need to *refresh my memory* on the subject of exchange rates and international trade.

23 I want to *deepen my understanding* of credit instruments and the market in commercial Bills.

24 I have a large file of a *customer's letters* and *have to find one* giving instructions to the bank on transferring money from deposit to current account.

B   Draw the table shown below on a sheet of A4 paper (sideways). Go through the list again with a fellow student, entering each of the reasons into the appropriate column of the table. You may add reasons of your own, if they are different from those in the list. Notice that the important part of each reason is in italics.

Overall reason	General reasons	Task orientated reasons	Personal interest reasons

Reading strategies

A   Study the following list of reading strategies which applies mainly to books:

I can read

1 every word in the book from cover to cover

2 the publisher's information only (i.e. the dust jacket, the title page and the publishing details)

3 the index only

4 the table of contents only

5 the first and last paragraph of each chapter

6 the first sentence of each paragraph

7 the main headings in the chapters only

8 the last paragraph of each chapter

9 only certain pages mentioned in the index

10 only certain sections that interest me

11 each chapter that contains anything I need to know

12 most of the book, but skipping certain chapters or sections that appear to be unimportant

NOTE You may also *invent* your own reading strategies similar to the ones above. But make sure they are realistic in terms of your reading aims.

B Work in pairs. Match the above list of strategies to the list of reading purposes in the previous section. One student can read out the reading purposes while the other checks the list of strategies to suggest one appropriate to the purpose. Then change lists and work the other way.

C Select reading strategies from the above list which would apply to newspaper articles connected with banking. You need to bring newspaper articles on financial, banking and economic topics to class.

D Assess a book for relevance to your reading purpose Bring a textbook and an essay question to class and be prepared to answer the questions below before your class or group. The rest of the group should be prepared to challenge your statement and you should be able to defend it by pointing out parts of the textbook as evidence.

1 Read out your essay question and analysis of the topics and functions.

2 Give the title of the textbook you have chosen to study to help you answer the essay question. Give
   a the name of the author and, if possible, his or her professional background. (This information should be found in the publisher's blurb on the dust jacket.)
   b the sub-title of the book, if any
   c the year of publication
   d where in the library it can be found, if it is a library book
   e information as to why you chose the book: was it recommended? your own selection? picked out at random?

3 Say what your reasons for reading the book are, both in terms of your personal reasons for reading and the topic analysis of your essay. These should be as detailed as possible. (Refer to your table of reasons for reading.)

4 Explain your reading strategy – exactly how you are going to read the book, which parts of it and why.

5 Will it be necessary to look up things in other books? If so, say what they are. Also give the titles of other books you would want to use and what topics you would need them for.

Extension

Inference

A   Making inferences means understanding things which are not directly stated by the writer but which emerge indirectly from the text. Look at these examples of specific conclusions drawn from general statements:

General statements	Specific inferences
1 Banks are closed over weekends.	We won't be able to take money out on Saturday.
2 There are only a few large clearing banks in Britain.	There isn't much choice when deciding which bank to use.
3 Staff turnover in that bank is very low.	The manager takes an interest in the people who work with him.
4 Country X has been importing more than it exports for a long time.	Its balance of payments is in deficit.

B   Now complete the specific inferences from the general statements below. Use as many words as you need:

1 Exchange control regulations have been abolished.	Money can be . . . without permission.
2 It is dangerous to carry large sums of money at night.	I expect he will have the sense to . . . at home.
3 These days a lot of people either won't or can't pay their debts.	You have to . . . in advance.
4 During the seventies there were a number of bank failures in Britain.	It is not surprising that the first comprehensive banking law . . .

C   Now look at the following examples of another kind of inference, that draws general conclusions from specific statements.

NOTE   The inference drawn is not necessarily true. Its truth depends on the quality of the evidence put forward to support it.

Specific statements	General inference
1 His flat was broken into five times last year.	Housebreaking is very common in his area.
2 From 1979–82 most of the banks made large profits.	Banks do well in times of high inflation.
3 A very large sum in used notes was stolen.	It must be easy to obtain information about the movement of cash about the country.
4 Bankruptcies and unemployment increased for three years.	The government's monetary policy was a failure.

D   Now complete the general inferences from the specific statements below:

1 I had to wait half an hour to be served.	Service in that bank . . .
2 The bank made me pay a commission in addition to their usual charge.	Nowadays the bank . . .

3 There were three mistakes in his monthly   . . .
statement.

4 The money supply increased as fast as before.   The high interest rates . . .

E   What can you infer from what the editor of *Your Business* magazine
wrote? Look again at the editor's replies to letters on pages 59–61.
Re-read what the editor wrote and complete the inferences. The first
two have been done for you:
a It would be less trouble for the firm if all the employees . . .
It would be less trouble for the firm if all the employees opened bank
accounts.
b The terms of bank deposits vary according to . . .
The terms of bank accounts vary according to the amount deposited.
c In countries where it takes longer to clear cheques . . .
d The customer using the night safe facility takes the risk of . . .
e It is no longer normal practice for banks to . . .
f It is worth while for a company to do as much of its buying as
possible in . . . since it can then pay its suppliers without the cost of
. . .
g The company may want to know what arrangements can be made for
sums less than . . .

F   Group work There are five more of the editor's replies to firms'
banking problems. Write your own inferences and compare them with
those of other members of the group.

G   Further practice Say which of the inferences listed on the right can
be drawn from the paragraphs below:

1 Banks have had a shock from the government comparable to the one given to building societies last week. They have been ordered to deduct tax at source from interest paid to savers.

a The building societies were ordered to pay more tax last week.
b At present, tax is not deducted at source from savings accounts.
c The government is attacking the banks.

2 It is likely to cause substantial changes in the highly competitive market for savings and will penalise the poorer depositors. A spokesman for the Committee of London Clearing Bankers said that the move would be 'robbing the poor to benefit the rich'.

a The government does not care about the poor.
b This is a deliberate move by the government to hurt the less well-off.
c The poor keep all their savings in the banks.

3 The change will be in the 1984 Finance Bill and will take effect from April, 1985. The decision by the Inland Revenue was sent by letter to the British Bankers' Association in the same way as the letter to the Building Societies last week, telling them that they would have to pay much more tax on their dealings in government stocks.

a The banks were consulted over this move.
b The banks were not consulted.
c Tax rules are made by the Inland Revenue (tax department) alone.
d Changes in tax law have to be passed by Parliament.

Self-assessment

A   Answer the questions below without looking back at the previous pages:

1 mark per question

1 The information in questions can be analysed into _____ information and requested information.
2 It is also important to understand the _____ , or what the question asks you to do.
3 Apart from analysing questions you need to have a clear idea of your own reading _____ .
4 When you have clearly understood the topics requested by the question, you should then decide what _____ to use for your reading task.
5 Where in a book can you usually find information about the professional interest and background of the author?
6 Where do you find the date of publication?
7 A cleared balance is
   a an account which is in credit
   b a current account which has been changed from being a deposit account
   c an amount from a cheque three days after it has been credited to the payee's account

True or false:
8 The majority of banks return cheques to their drawers automatically.
9 UK banks issue cheque cards allowing their holders to withdraw £75 in banks on the continent.
10 The main problem with issuing cheques to be cashed is
   a security of the cheque
   b identification of the payee
   c the signature of the drawer

Decide which function best describes what the following expressions do:
11 Your best course of action is to . . .
   a advising   **b** comparing   **c** informing
12 A night safe is a safe built into the outside wall of a bank for the use of . . .
   a instructing   **b** informing   **c** defining

B   Now check your answers in the Answer Key and award yourself marks out of a total of 12. Try to understand your mistakes, if you made any.

Unit 7   The creation of money

Interior of a Goldsmith's shop

Preview

New items in this unit are

1 distinguishing the main point in a paragraph from supporting detail

2 studying notes on a subject and completing them from a text

3 practising several ways of getting at the meanings of words in texts

4 expressing sequence in reports containing series of events

5 the creation of money by the goldsmith bankers in England 300 years ago

You will also practise surveying the text before reading, guessing meanings, asking and answering questions, defending your own interpretation of a text, understanding simple balance sheets and evaluating your progress at the end of the unit.

Preparing to read

Surveying the SCOPE

A   Survey the *subject* of the text: the creation of money. Write down two or three questions to ask your fellow students, to determine how much they already know, e.g.

1 What do you know about the creation of money?
2 How do the banks create money?
3 Does the creation of money mean that more notes are printed?
4 Does the creation of money meant that more coins are minted?
5 What is bank money?
6 How does the government create money?
Ask and answer the questions.

B   Survey the *coverage*. The passage you are about to study comes from the book *Money: theory, policy and institutions* (2nd edition), by Andrew Crockett, Van Nostrand Reinhold, 1979. Study the Contents page at the top of the next page as a preparation for understanding the coverage and writer's purpose.

1 In which section of the book *Money* does the passage in this unit appear?
2 Judging by the Table of Contents, what aspects of money creation does the text deal with? economic? historical? banking? accounting? manufacturing?

C   Survey also all *examples* of *illustrations* that accompany the text you are about to read. Look at the drawing at the beginning of this unit. It does not appear in Crockett's book but it was drawn at the time of the goldsmiths. The drawing shows a goldsmith in the dress of a respectable

London merchant of the sixteenth century. The animal is a griffin, a mythological beast with unusual characteristics. And the words are clear in spite of the old letters and spelling.

1 What was the value of such a symbol as the griffin?
2 What does he mean by *use*?
3 What is the *principal*?
4 Can you recognise the objects on the table?

Contents page

The passage   *The creation of money*

A   Read the first and last sentences of each paragraph as fast as possible to get the gist of the passage. Read anything else that catches your eye.

B   Read through the questions in the table on page 73.

C   Then read the passage more slowly, bearing in mind the questions you have just read.

Numbers in brackets refer to lines in the passage.

1 *emergence* (1) = rising up? sinking? meeting together? (see *submerge, merger*)

2 *physical* (2) Why does the author use italics?

3 What is the inference in *still represented title to gold* (3–4)? Did this situation continue?

pari passu (4) = in equal proportion

4 *effected* (6) = carried out? replaced? substituted?

5 *net withdrawals* (7–8) = all the withdrawals? minor withdrawals?

6 *With more and more . . . holding* (5–9)
a note holdings were increasing?
b gold holdings were increasing?
c withdrawals were increasing?

7 *contemplated* (10) = thought about? counted up? calculated the amount of?

8 *custody* (12) = keeping? investment? handling?

9 Find a synomyn for *custody*. (19–25)

10 *impecunious* (14) = poor? rich? happy?

11 *usurious* (14): meaning? (see *use, usury*)

12 *this combination of circumstances* (16) refers to:
a the previous sentence?
b the previous two sentences?
c everything in the paragraph up to that point?

13 Lines 19–20: a 'signpost' sentence. It points out what the author is going to do next. What words show this?

14 *assets* (25) = **a** valuables owed by the goldsmiths?
b valuables owed to the goldsmiths?

15 *liabilities* (25) = **a** valuables owed by the goldsmiths?
b valuables owed to the goldsmiths?

16 Lines 36–38: We can therefore infer that there is no increase in goldsmiths' —————— either.

17 Is the £100 (37) a *liability* of the goldsmiths or a liability of their customers?

D   Work through the passage again and answer the questions on the left.

With the emergence of the goldsmith-bankers, gold ceased to be the principal *physical* medium of exchange. However, although paper might circulate, it still represented title to gold and was matched *pari passu* by coin and bullion
5   lying in the goldsmiths' vaults. With more and more transactions being effected by means of bearer notes, or the writing of cheques, the goldsmiths realized that the net withdrawals from their stocks of gold were becoming very small in relation to the total amount they were holding. As
10   they contemplated the gold lying in their vaults, it naturally occurred to them that they could make more profit from it than simply fees received for safe custody. They were sitting on vast quantities of idle wealth, at the same time as impecunious individuals were paying usurious rates of
15   interest to money-lenders. Modern banking began when the goldsmiths exploited this combination of circumstances and began to lend out part of their holdings of gold against the promise to repay with interest.

This was an important step, and it is worth pausing to
20   spell out in more detail the sequence of events that occurs. Let us assume goldsmiths' customers had, in total, entrusted £1000 worth of gold to their safe keeping. Before they undertook any lending, the combined balance sheet of goldsmiths would be as follows:

25 | *Liabilities* | *Assets* |
| --- | --- |
| Gold deposits £1000 | Gold coin and bullion £1000 |
| £1000 | £1000 |

Now assume that the goldsmiths decided to use the gold lying idle in their vaults, to make loans at interest. They
30   lend £100 to a borrower, who takes his loan in the form of gold. The balance sheet is now as follows:

Liabilities	*Assets*	
Gold deposits £1000	Gold coin and bullion	£900
	Loans to customers	100
35 | £1000 | | £1000 |

There has been no increase in goldsmiths' liabilities, but there is an increase of £100 in gold circulating outside the goldsmiths' vaults. When the borrower uses this gold to acquire goods and services, the likelihood is that the re-
40   ceivers of the money will deposit what they receive back with the goldsmiths. When this happens, the balance sheet would be this:

18 Third balance sheet (43): How much of the *liabilities* is physical gold?

19 How much of the *assets* is physical gold?

20 *claims* (47) = gold? deposits? assets?

21 Would all the goldsmiths have had the same amount of *physical gold*?

22 Line 51: What *process* is the author talking about here?

23 *deposit receipts* (52) = banknotes? statements of account? cheques?

24 The system depended most on
  a goldsmiths trusting each other's honesty and square dealing?
  b goldsmiths trusting each other's judgement of the people they lent money to?
  c the borrowers always keeping enough gold on deposit to cover their withdrawals?

25 *settle* (60) = pay? account for? accept?

	Liabilities	*Assets*
45	Gold deposits £1100	Gold coin and bullion £1000
		Loans to customers 100
	£1100	£1100

The total quantity of deposits – that is to say, claims which can in theory be turned into gold on demand – has in-
50 creased without any increase in the quantity of physical gold.

The next stage in this process is for the goldsmith to issue deposit receipts, not just against the delivery of physical gold, but against gold certificates. If an individual pays for goods with a cheque drawn on goldsmith A, and the seller
55 of the goods takes the cheque to goldsmith B, goldsmith B will be quite willing to accept it so long as he has confidence in goldsmith A. He may ask goldsmith A to settle the indebtedness by a transfer of gold, but on the other hand he may be quite content to have a claim on A which he can use
60 to settle a debt with C, D or E at some future date. With this refinement, the goldsmith, our pioneer banker, is enabled to 'create' money by a simple book entry, without a single coin being moved.

Discussion

A   Ask and answer questions as follows:

What	was / were	the	the principal medium of exchange at the time of the emergence of the goldsmiths? principal store of value at that time? relationship of paper money to gold? functions of the goldsmiths before they started lending? combination of circumstances which the goldsmiths exploited? important steps taken by the goldsmiths? first effect of lending? final effect of lending? result of lending? next stage in the process? advantage of not immediately demanding coin for gold certificates?

What happened	with the emergence of the goldsmith bankers? to paper money at that time? to the gold deposits in the hands of the goldsmiths? to gold coin at that time? to the gold lent out by the goldsmiths? to the total amount of money stock? next? when an individual drew a cheque?

B   Ask and answer other questions of your own about the passage.

C   Which of the following would you put forward as the two most important to the creation of money? Be prepared to defend your answer.

1 the need to find a safe place where gold could be deposited
2 the existence of usurious rates of interest charged by moneylenders
3 the willingness of goldsmiths to accept receipts from other goldsmiths for gold deposits
4 the possession of safe strong rooms by the goldsmiths in London
5 fees received for safe custody of gold
6 the custom of issuing gold-paying bearer notes
7 the use of cheques
8 the confidence that existed in the goldsmiths' honesty and good faith

D   True or false? Write *true* or *false* for each of the following:

1 A banker's liabilities consist of all loans and deposits from customers.
2 A banker's assets consist of all loans and deposits from customers.
3 A banker's liabilities consist of his holdings of gold and loans to customers.
4 A banker's assets consist of his holdings of gold and loans to customers.

E   Copy out and complete this balance sheet with one word for each blank:

1 _____		**2** _____	
gold deposits	£1,100	gold coin and **4** _____	£1,000
3 _____ of gold certificates	100	loans of **5** _____ certificates to customers	100
		gold **6** _____	100
7 _____		**8** _____	

Analysis

Expressing sequence

A   The reading passage 'The Creation of Money' describes a historical process which is shown by a sequence of events. Study the different ways of showing sequence. Numbers in brackets refer to lines in the passage:

1 With the emergence of the goldsmith bankers, (1) . . .

2 With more and more transactions being effected by means of bearer notes, or the writing of cheques, (5–7) . . .

3 The next stage in this process (51) . . .

4 With this refinement, (60–61) . . .

These could also be written like this:

1 When the goldsmith bankers emerged, . . .

2 While more and more cheques were being effected by . . .

3 Next, . . .

4 Following this step, . . .

B   When you want to describe a sequence of events, you can use expressions like the ones above, but they must be followed by a subject and main verb. Look at the table below:

Sequencing word, + Main sentence phrase or clause		
	subject	**+ main verb + complement**
First,	a cheque	is drawn.
Then,	it	is given to the payee.
Next,	the payee	deposits it in her bank.
After that,	the payee's bank	credits the amount of the cheque to the payee's account.

C   Now complete the paragraph below with one word for each space:

Opening a bank account

First, **1** _____ which bank will provide the best service. Then, **2** _____ there are several banks near your home, decide which one **3** _____ the most convenient for you to use. Next, **4** _____ will need to call at the bank, preferably **5** _____ they are not too busy, and give them **6** _____ name and address and samples of your signature. **7** _____ that, the bank will send you a cheque **8** _____ and a bank card.

'I'm sorry if the check is a little wet. My husband was crying.'

D   Complete the following paragraph by writing down one of the words from the list below for each space:

when, buyer, until, gold, from, became, he

Money and gold

1 _____ the invention by Italian bankers of Bills of Exchange, **2** _____ had to be moved from place to place to pay for trade. **3** _____ that time onwards paper credits **4** _____ more important in Europe. **5** _____ a merchant wanted to be paid for goods **6** _____ would issue an order in writing for the amount to be paid by his customer. The **7** _____ would accept the Bill by signing it and returning it to the seller.

E   Now find the expressions at the top of the next page in the reading passage and write down the subject and main verb following each one. The first two have been done for you:

	Main sentence		
Sequencing clause or phrase	**subject**	**+**	**main verb**
1 As they contemplated the gold lying in their vaults . . .	it		occurred to
2 . . . at the same time as individuals were paying interest to moneylenders	They		were sitting on
3 . . . when the goldsmiths exploited this combination of circumstances . . .	———		———
4 Before they undertook any lending . . .	———		———
5 When the borrower uses gold to acquire goods and services . . .	———		———
6 When this happens, . . .	———		———

F Now rewrite the following passage, converting the words in brackets into sequencing clauses like the examples in **A** to **E** above:

1 (growth of the money markets in the 1970s), an increasing number of 'fringe' banks were set up. Some of them depended entirely on one side of the market such as property or equity shares. **2** (time went on) some of these banks failed because they lent too much to single sectors and became dependent on them. **3** (the collapse of the property market in 1974) one bank, which had invested all its depositors' money in property, collapsed with it. **4** (the 1970s) the Authorities in London set up the Deposit Protection Fund and all the banks were asked to pay money into it. **5** (the scheme was first proposed) most of the large banks protested. They said the scheme was just a way of protecting bad banks **6** (they were short of funds).

Subordinate clauses

A It occurred to them that . . . Study the grammar of the following sentences:

Main sentence			**Subordinate clause**		
subject	**verb**		**subject**	**verb**	
It	occurred to them	that	they	could make	more profit from it.
We	can assume	that	the goldsmiths' customers	had	£1,000.
Now [you]	assume	that	the goldsmiths	decided to use	the gold.
The likelihood	is	that	the receivers of the money	will deposit	it with the goldsmith.

Notice that both the main part of the sentence and the subordinate clause have verbs.

B Complete the sentences below, following the pattern in the table above:

1 Historians have realised that modern banking . . . with the emergence of . . . .

2 The goldsmiths understood that this combination . . . them an opportunity to increase their wealth.

3 We can safely assume that paper . . . an acceptable medium of exchange.

4 The early bankers had to be sure that their customers . . . reliable and honest.

5 The system worked because anyone holding a bank note knew that he . . . on demand.

6 The new president promised that the country's debts . . .

7 The Chancellor of the Exchequer said that . . . the burden of taxation.

8 The government announced . . . (interest rates)

9 The new leaders declared that . . . (the country's problems)

10 When I went to see him the manager informed me . . . (the goods/returned)

Extension

Note-making practice

The passage 'Confidence without Gold', which follows, is the continuation of the passage 'The Creation of Money' in Crockett's book.

A   Read the passage very quickly, in the usual way, to get the gist of it. Then read it more thoroughly.

B   Answer the questions on the left.

C   Study the analysis of the text which follows. Then complete the model notes by supplying one word for each space.

D   Make your own notes on the entire text. Follow a pattern like this:

1. Main heading
   a. supporting point
   b. supporting point
   c. suporting point etc.

2. Main heading
   a. supporting point etc.

E   Remember you have to use these notes for revision before exams, so set them out clearly with plenty of space.

F   To save yourself time, use abbreviations, signs and symbols such as ∴, ∵, &, = to show the logical relationship of ideas in the passage.

Numbers in brackets refer to line numbers.

1 What do such *claims* (2) take the form of?

2 Identify the words referred to by the words in **bold** type.

3 Whose *confidence* (4)?

Confidence without Gold

A monetary system based on banks depends on the acceptability of claims which are not fully backed by gold. Confidence, as we have seen, is of the essence. Every banker is subject to the overriding requirement to retain confidence

4 *redeem* (5) = pay back? service? accept?

5 What *bitter experiences* (7)? This refers forward to sentences 6, 7 & 8.

6 *crises of confidence* (12) = danger zones? periods of acute lack of trust? high risk borrowers?

7 Which word indicates that careful bankers were strong enough for *most* crises of confidence?

8 Which word indicates that sentence 6 is in contrast with sentence 7?

criteria (19) = laws, banking principles

9 Find a word synonymous with *insolvent*.

10 Give a definition of *bankrupt* (20) and of *illiquid* (21).

11 Why should a bank want to change some of its assets into gold at short notice?

12 *one bank of unquestioned solidity* (23–24) refers forward to what?

13 Was the Bank of England the central bank?

14 Who does *Psychologically* (35) refer to?

15 What would a customer have handed in to the bank to get gold?

16 *adverse* (50) = favourable? unfavourable? reasonable?

5   in his ability to redeem his liabilities. This means **he** must keep capital reserves and liquid assets. With time, and many bitter experiences, the banking system came to a general view on how much capital reserve was needed to run a deposit-banking business and what proportion of
10   liquid assets should be held to ensure the ability to meet depositors' requirements. Even prudent bankers, however, were not immune to *all* crises of confidence.[6] In a serious financial crash, every bank came under suspicion, and since no bank kept 100% of **its** assets in the form of
15   gold, all were exposed to some risk.[7]

In London, in the early nineteenth century, there were a number of quite spectacular financial crashes in which banks which were being prudently run according to accepted criteria were pushed into insolvency, not because
20   they were actually bankrupt (with liabilities in excess of assets) but because they were illiquid (unable to convert some of their assets into gold at short notice). It therefore came to be suggested that one bank, of unquestioned solidity, should act to support the rest of the financial system.
25   This **it** could do by 'rediscounting' (i.e. buying) the assets of those banks which were short of ready cash. In London, the bank which emerged to fill **this** role was the Bank of England. Since **this** became the central bank of the system (though the term 'central bank' did not come into general
30   usage until much later) the other banks gradually ceased to hold gold and centralized **their** cash reserves in holdings of notes and balances at the Bank of England.

At **this** stage in the development of money it was still an important aspect of bank balances that they were conver-
35   tible into gold. Psychologically, gold represented the true store of value which backed the paper assets which, for the sake of convenience, were the principal medium of exchange. People knew from experience that banks could fail, and the criterion by which they judged a bank's sound-
40   ness was its ability to supply gold to honour its promise to pay.

As the 19th century wore on, however, there were a number of developments which tended to reduce the importance of gold in the system. In the first place, the in-
45   creased security of the banking system resulting from the gradual assumption by the Bank of England of responsibility for financial stability reduced the fear of banking crashes. Secondly, the growth of banks was much more rapid than the growth of the Bank of England's gold stock,
50   and there were **no serious adverse consequences**. By the outbreak of World War I, gold had diminished consider-

17 *suspended* (53) = hung? stopped completely? stopped temporarily?

ably in importance and, during the war, the Bank of England suspended its promise to convert its notes into gold. It became apparent that the promise to convert into
55 gold was unnecessary to the acceptability of **paper money**. So long as there was confidence in the financial system, paper money could exist without any backing of gold.

The fact that there is now no physical gold backing to money does not mean, however, that **it** is unbacked. A
60 bank's assets must exceed its deposit liabilities or else it is insolvent. And it is the assets of a bank which form the backing for money. These assets are a fairly heterogeneous collection, of notes, coins, short-term bills, longer-term investments and advances to customers. These assets
65 represent claims on present or future resources and are just as real and valuable as a gold bar – more so since they produce an interest return.

18 So liabilities are backed by _____ ?

19 *heterogeneous* (62) = similar? rich? varied?

20 *advances* (64) = loans? deposits? advice?

Text analysis
A monetary system based on banks depends on the acceptability of claims:

– importance of confidence
– bankers must be able to honour claims in gold
– hard experience showed what proportion of assets needed to be kept liquid and as capital reserve

Model notes (Supply one word for each space.)
But even (1)_____ bankers were exposed to risk
– in (2)_____ crises everyone was suspect
– no bank (3)_____ 100% of its assets in gold

Bank (4)_____ of the early 19th c.
– ∴ insolvency not (5)_____
– insolvency arose from lack of liquidity

∴ Need (6)_____ one standby bank which had to (7)_____
– of unquestioned solidity
– always able to (8)_____ assets such as Bills to enable (9)_____ to obtain liquid assets
– capable of holding (10)_____ reserves of all banks
This role (11)_____ taken by the Bank of England *but* (12)_____ wasn't seen as a central bank yet.

Continue writing notes in the same way.

Self-assessment

A   Answer the questions.

marks

1 What is implied by having *the use* of a sum of money?
a getting interest
b being able to lend it
c being able to borrow it   (1)

2 What does SCOPE stand for in terms of pre-reading survey?   (5)

3 Why did gold become less important during the nineteenth century?
a The commercial banks stopped being interested in it as a commodity.
b Most of the banks' gold reserves were kept in the Bank of England.
c There was enough confidence in the banking system without it.   (1)

4 Why are modern banking assets more valuable than gold?
   a They represent productive wealth.
   b The price of gold is unstable.
   c They have less gold than other assets.   (1)

5 How could a bank be insolvent but not bankrupt?
   a It hasn't got enough cash.
   b Its total cash is more than its assets.
   c Its withdrawals are greater than its deposits.   (1)

6 Complete the following:
   a _____ banking started, bankers' main activities were money-changing and transferring payments. **b** _____ , in medieval times, bankers in Italy started to lend out surplus funds which they had on deposit. **c** _____ this happened, banking as we know it today started.   (3)

7 Convert the following into sentences:
   a . . . the increasing use of convertible paper money, . . . banks . . . difficult to pay gold on demand.   (6)
   b . . . banks . . . facing liquidity problems, the need for a central bank . . . clear.   (6)

8 Convert the following groups of words into sentences:
   a Customers must be confident that (their banks/cash on demand)   (3)
   b All bankers must appear to be capable of redeeming their debts when they fall due. This means that (capital reserves/liquid assets)   (3)

9 Make the following into complete sentences:
   a During the crisis people suspected that _____ (banks/gold/notes)   (5)
   b They received a letter from their bank telling them that _____ (overdraft/exceed/limit)   (5)

Total (40)

B   Check your answers in the Answer Key and make a note of your score.

Unit 8   Graphs and tables

Preview

This unit is about understanding and extracting information from graphs and tables of figures. There is also some writing practice.

Reading graphs and tables

Comparing figures

A Study the table and answer the questions.

Foreign Trade of India*
(Merchandise only: Private and Govt.)   *(Rs. Crores)*

Year/Quarter	Import	Export†	Balance of trade
1961–62	1,091.63	660.58	− 431.05
1965–66	1,408.52	805.64	− 602.88
1968–69	1,910.20	1,357.78	− 552.42
1969–70	1,582.10	1,413.27	− 168.83
1970–71	1,634.20	1,535.16	− 99.04
1971–72	1,824.54	1,608.22	− 216.32
1972–73	1,867.44	1,970.83	+ 103.39
1973–74	2,955.37	2,523.40	− 435.97
1974–75	4,518.78	3,328.83	−1189.95
1975–76	5,265.22	4,042.81	−1222.41
1976–77	5,074.00	5,146.00	+ 72.00
1977–78	6.025.00	5,404.00	− 621.00
1978–79	6,814.00	5,726.00	−1088.00
1979–80	8,908.00	6,459.00	−2449.00
1980–81‡	12,210.16	6,675.15	−5535.01
1981–82‡ April to June	2,815.25	1,652.04	−1163.21

1 crore = 10,000,000 rupees

* Figures include land, sea, air-borne trade of India.
† Include re-exports.
‡ Provisional.

1 What kind of exports and imports does this table *not* deal with?

2 Which year saw the smallest deficit?

3 Which year saw the largest deficit?

4 Which year saw the biggest change in the balance of trade position, not counting 1981?

5 From the figures, was 1976–77
    a a comparatively good year?
    b much better than the previous few years?
    c just as bad as the previous years?
    d much worse than the previous years?

6 Which of the following are reasons why the trade gap has been getting steadily wider in the last few years?
    a steadily decreasing exports
    b steadily increasing imports
    c sudden increases in imports
    d irregular exports

B   When the figures for the whole year were in, would you expect the balance of trade figures for 1981–82 to have shown a larger or smaller deficit than in 1980–81?

Information from tables

Using the information shown in the table, make sentences about the trade gap, following the examples:

A   The trade balance
example
In 1965–66 the trade gap increased by 1,718.3 million rupees to Rs. 6,028.8 million.
In 1968–69 the trade gap decreased by 504.6 million rupees to Rs. 5,524.2 million.

1 In 1969–70 . . .
2 In 1970–71 . . .
3 In 1971–72 . . .
4 In 1972–73 there was a trade surplus of . . .
5 In 1976–77 the trade gap of . . . was into a surplus of . . . .
6 In 1978–79 . . .
7 In 1973–74 the trade surplus of the previous year was turned into a deficit of . . .
8 In 1976–77 . . .

B   Imports and exports compared
example
In 1961–62 imports exceeded exports by Rs. 4,310.5 million.

1 In 1965–66 . . .
2 In 1972–73 . . .
3 In 1976–77 . . .

C   Comparing the trade balances of different years
example
The trade gap widened in 1965–66 by 1,718.3 million rupees to Rs. 6,028.8 million.
The trade gap narrowed in 1968–69 by 504.6 million rupees to Rs. 5,524.2 million.

1 (1969–70)
2 (1971–72)
3 (1979–80)

Understanding graphs

A   Study the line graph of Indian exports and imports on page 82.

B   Answer the following questions:

1 What does Rs. stand for?

2 The vertical lines show:
   a 31st December–1st January of each year
   b the volume of goods, exported and imported
   c the division between exports and imports
   d the points at which the values of trade are given

Foreign Trade of India (Merchandise only: Private and Govt.)

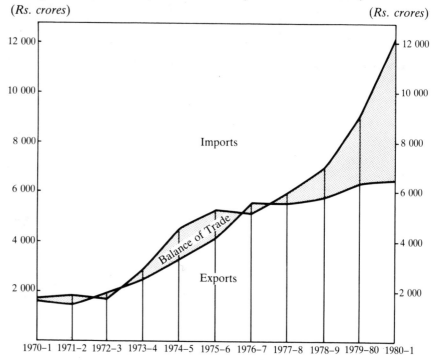

3 True or false:
  a From 1971 to 1976 the value of exports increased steadily.
  b In 1971–2 there was a trade surplus.
  c In 1976–7 there was a surplus.
  d Imports peaked in 1975–6.
  e Exports peaked in 1976–7.
  f Imports increased at an even rate.

4 What are the advantages of a graph like this over the table of figures?

5 What are the advantages of the table of figures for showing exports and imports?

Information from graphs

Using the information in the line-graph, make sentences about the imports and exports of India, using the following expressions:

increased/rose/climbed   steadily/sharply/gradually/steeply
levelled off
decreased slightly/showed a slight decrease
large/small/moderate/huge/growing   trade deficit/surplus

examples
In the year 1972–3 imports decreased slightly while exports rose gradually, producing a healthy trade surplus.
In the year 1974–5 imports rose sharply while exports increased only gradually, producing a large trade deficit.

1 (1975–6) In the year . . .
2 (1976–7)
3 (1977–8)
4 (1980–1)

More on graphic information

A   The Motor Giants Study Tables A, B, C and D on pages 84–85 until you are familiar with the kind of information they contain. Then answer the questions below:

Which table (A, B, C or D)
1 compares exports of Toyota cars with those of other Japanese cars?   (   )
2 projects future car demand over the whole world?   (   )
3 compares domestic production with overseas production?   (   )
4 shows the proportion of total Toyota car sales in different parts of the world?   (   )
5 compares passenger car demand with demand for non-passenger cars?   (   )
6 compares the total car imports from Japan in each area of the world?   (   )
7 shows the production of the four largest motor manufacturers in the world?   (   )
8 shows the production of overseas manufacturing plants?   (   )
9 shows the proportion of Toyotas exported to North America that is exported to the USA?   (   )
10 compares car demand in different parts of the world?   (   )

B   Table A: A Statistical Table Read this and the following tables in detail and write down the answers in your notebook:
NOTE   KDs are *k*nock *d*own cars, i.e. car kits exported for assembly abroad.

1 How many cars did Volkswagen produce in Germany in 1973?
2 In which year did GM overseas plants produce the largest number of cars?
3 In which years did Ford overseas factories produce more than their US factories?
4 According to the table, can you assume that Toyotas are assembled outside Japan? Why?
5 Reading the totals of each manufacturer from left to right, what has Toyota succeeded in doing which none of the other companies has done?
6 In which year did Toyota's production overtake the domestic production of Ford?
7 Which years were the worst, in terms of drops in production, for GM? Ford? Volkswagen? Toyota?

C   Table B: The Bar Graph
1 Which part of the world is the biggest market for Japanese cars?
2 How many Japanese cars were exported to Latin America in 1981?
3 Which part of Europe imported most cars from Japan?
4 Which part of the world imported more Toyotas than everywhere else except North America?
5 How many cars did Toyota export in 1981?

D   Table C: The Pie Graph
1 What proportion of Toyota exports went to Southeast Asia in 1981?
2 Which region was the third largest importer of Toyotas in 1981?
3 What percentage of Toyota exports went to Europe outside the EEC?

E   Table D: The Map Graph
1 What was the total number of cars sold in the world in 1979?
2 What increase in sales is projected for 1990?
3 Which region has the smallest projected increase in market size?
4 Which region has the largest projected increase in market size?
5 Which regions show a market size of less than a million in 1979?

Table A

Car Production by World's Largest Automakers (In 1,000 Cars)										
		1973	1974	1975	1976	1977	1978	1979	1980	1981
General Motors	Domestic	6,512	4,678	4,658	6,218	6,695	6,878	6,445	4,771	4,611
	Overseas	2,172	2,012	1,971	2,350	2,373	2,604	1,848	2,330	2,151
	Total	8,684	6,690	6,629	8,568	9,068	9,482	8,293	7,101	6,762
Ford Motor	Domestic	3,772	3,328	2,677	3,214	3,971	4,090	3,227	2,151	2,102
	Overseas	2,099	1,931	1,901	2,090	2,451	2,371	2,579	2,178	2,211
	Total	5,871	5,259	4,578	5,304	6,422	6,461	5,806	4,328	4,313
Volks-wagen	Domestic	1,720	1,359	1,229	1,436	1,561	1,569	1,558	1,932	1,894
	Overseas	615	709	720	730	658	816	984	562	385
	Total	2,335	2,068	1,949	2,166	2,219	2,385	2,542	2,494	2,279
Toyota … Total		**2,308**	**2,115**	**2,336**	**2,488**	**2,721**	**2,929**	**3,073**	**3,380**	**3,333**

Note: KDs are included in Toyota's production.

Table B

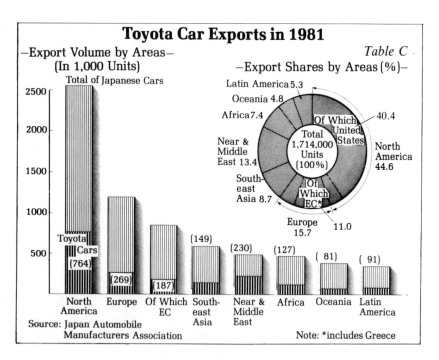

Toyota Car Exports in 1981

—Export Volume by Areas—
(In 1,000 Units)

Table C

—Export Shares by Areas (%)—

Source: Japan Automobile Manufacturers Association

Note: *includes Greece

Table D

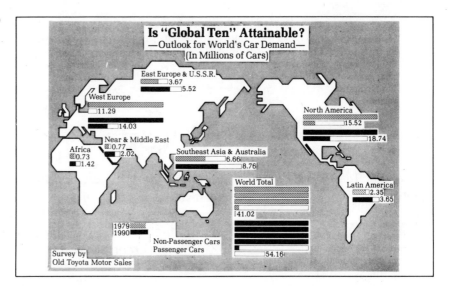

Writing from graphs and tables

A report

Using information from tables to complete a report

A   Complete the following report with figures, and names of countries and regions, taken from tables A, B, C and D. Car production figures should be written out in full, e.g. 2,308 on the table will be written 2,308,000.

Toyota aims at a major increase in market share

Recent reports of a joint venture between Toyota Motor Corporation and General Motors of the USA have aroused considerable interest in the automobile industry. With a total output of (1)_____ in 1981, Toyota can claim to be the (2)_____ largest motor manufacturer in the world, if one discounts the (3)_____ production of Ford. Of a world output of (4)_____ in 1979 Toyota produced 7.5% or (5)_____ cars and it is the avowed aim of the company to raise this share of the market to a 'global (6)_____%'.

Clearly, Toyota's largest single market is the (7)_____ which imported (8)_____ vehicles from Toyota in 1981. This is more than was imported by the next three largest regions together, namely (9)_____ (10) the _____ and _____ _____ and Southeast (11)_____ . There are several reasons why Toyota is concentrating so much attention on the USA. One of these is the projected increase in the size of the US market – (12)_____ vehicles by 1990 compared with (13)_____ in Europe. But in Europe competition from local (14)_____ as well as the European plants of GM and Ford is intense. In the USA, on the other hand, GM and Ford output has declined since (15)_____ and only recently have these two firms introduced small cars to compete with those of (16)_____ .

The other area with big potential is (17)_____ _____ whose 1979 sales were 6,660,000 cars which is projected to increase by (18)_____ in 1990. Moreover 90% of the market there is already Japanese.

B Complete the two following passages with one word, abbreviation or figure for each numbered space. Write down the answers in your notebook. (More than one answer is possible.) Make sure you survey the titles before you start reading and writing.

Country Report
SINGAPORE

By Arthur Tan Nee Kiam and Barun Roy

When J. Y. M. Pillary, chairman of the Development Bank of Singapore, said last March that, for the DBS Group, the year 1981 was 'reasonably satisfactory', he was clearly making an understatement. Behind this 'reasonably satisfactory' success lies the story of a tooth-and-nail battle that brought (1)_____ to the top as Singapore's fastest (2)_____ bank.

It nudged out first placer (3)_____ to emerge ahead of the rest with end-1981 total assets of (4)_____ million. In doing this, it pulled off a creditable 57% growth over 1980, against UOB's 29.4%, Overseas-Chinese (5)_____ Corporation's 27.4%, and Overseas Union Bank's 32.9%.

At the same time, OCBC lost to (6)_____ its traditional place of honour as the bank with the biggest net profit. (7)_____ even fell behind UOB to rank third among the (8) S_____ Big Four. It chalked up S\$88.12 million against DBS's (9)_____ million and (10)_____'s S\$91.18 million. In terms of the rate of (11)_____ profit growth, it fared even worse with a record of 30.9%, after 64.9% for DBS, 57.7% for UOB, and 50.3% for (12)_____ .

The story of a new style in reserves and resources managment

DBS fights its way to the top

Among the Big Four, the redoubtable OCBC has slipped down to third place in terms of both total assets and net profits, while DBS has emerged on top. Showing remarkable aggressiveness, UOB has crept up to the second slot.

The fight for profits
(amounts in S\$ million)

	1981 Amount	Rank	1980 Amount	Rank	1979 Amount	Rank
DBS	103.09	1	62.5	2	39.5	2
UOB	91.18	2	57.8	3	38.0	3
OCBC	88.12	3	67.3	1	44.8	1
OUB	44.36	4	29.5	4	19.5	4

Note: Figures relate to profit after tax for parent banks.

How the Big Four fared
(amounts in S\$ million)
By total assets (incl. contra items)

	1981 Amount	Rank	1980 Amount	Rank	1979 Amount	Rank
DBS	11,271.1	1	7,182.5	2	5,488.7	2
UOB	9,673.2	2	7,474.6	1	6,276.1	1
OCBC	7,019.6	3	5,508.5	3	5,188.3	3
OUB	4,808.3	4	3,617.9	4	3,241.7	4

By total loans and advances

	1981	Rank	1980	Rank	1979	Rank
DBS	4,513.0	1	3,031.7	2	1,832.5	2
UOB	3,675.5	2	3,137.8	1	2,461.3	1
OCBC	2,525.1	3	2,147.6	3	1,758.4	3
OUB	2,185.7	4	1,802.7	4	1,361.4	4

By total deposits

	1981	Rank	1980	Rank	1979	Rank
UOB	5,341.8	1	4,377.8	1	3,762.3	1
DBS	4,621.8	2	3,039.9	3	2,055.9	3
OCBC	4,475.1	3	3,760.0	2	3,616.0	2
OUB	3,520.7	4	2,970.0	4	1,918.2	4

Note: the figures relate to group accounts.

Innovative role

Run by a (13)_____ of young and daring executives imbued with
unbounded enthusiasm and dynamism, DBS has been universally
acclaimed as an (14)_____ bank and as a pioneer in (15)_____
untrodden paths. Today it is the undisputed (16)_____ in the field of
investment banking in (17)_____ .

Last year, for example, DBS managed . . . In all, it accounted for
. . . In addition, it co-managed . . .

OCBC, the banking colossus which this year (18)_____ its 50th
anniversary, was evidently paying the (19)_____ for its steadfast
conservatism. While DBS and (20)_____ continued to show strong
(21)_____ in profitability and (22)_____ maintained its rate,
(23)_____'s growth rate slipped conspicuously from its 50% record in
1980.

Displaying a remarkable degree of aggressiveness, (24)_____ moved
one rung up to the second spot in profitability at the end of 1981.
(25)_____ , it would still find it difficult to wrestle with DBS for the
(26)_____ position in 1982.

C   Cocoa survey Study the Nigerian agricultural exports tables and the
cocoa production graph that follow:

Contribution of major crops to total exports
(per cent)

	1960	1968	1972	1975	1977	1978	1979	1980
Cocoa	22.2	10.0	3.0	2.7	7.7	6.2	4.1	2.2
Palm kernels	15.7	6.1	1.0	0.7	0.4	0.2	0.1	0.1
Palm oil	8.4	2.3	0.5	0.1	—	—	—	—
Groundnut oil	3.2	1.5	0.4	0.2	—	—	—	—
Groundnuts	13.8	6.4	0.8	0.1	—	—	—	—
Cotton	3.7	1.1	...	...	0.1	0.1	—	—
Rubber	8.6	2.5	0.9	0.6	0.2	0.2	0.1	0.1
Beniseed	1.1	1.0	0.3	0.1	—	—	—	—
Total	**76.7**	**30.9**	**6.9**	**4.5**	**8.4**	**6.7**	**4.3**	**2.4**

Source: Central Bank of Nigeria

Exports of agricultural commodities
('000 tons)

	1946	1970	1971	1972	1973	1974	1975	1976	1977	1978	1979	1980
Cocoa	102	196	256	228	214	179	175	219	168	192	218	157
Palm kernels	282	185	242	212	137	184	171	272	186	57	51	50
Palm oil	103	8	19	2	—	—	11	3	—	3	—	—
Groundnuts	290	291	137	106	198	28	—	2	1	—	—	—
Groundnut oil	...	90	43	40	107	28	—	—	—	—	—	—

Note: Palm oil and groundnut exports virtually ceased in the mid-1970s.

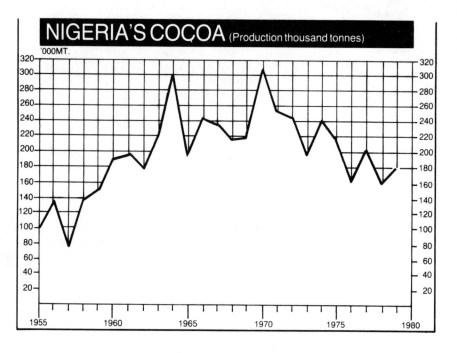

NIGERIA'S COCOA (Production thousand tonnes)

D   Use the tables below to write ten true statements about the graph at the top of the page:

There	was has been	a an	substantial overall steady general gradual sharp steep spectacular slow rapid	increase decrease fall rise recovery improvement decline upturn downturn	in the	production output	of cocoa in Nigeria	in . . . since . . . before . . . up to . . . after . . .
				recovery of				
			peak trough					

Now write another ten:

| Nigerian cocoa production | increased decreased fell rose recovered improved declined | substantially steadily spectacularly gradually sharply steeply | in the in between | last ten years seventies fifties first ten years 1964 1970 19— and 19— | and thereafter it . . . |
| | made an upturn saw a downturn peaked/troughed | | | | |

Check your sentences with your teacher or with fellow students.

Further writing from tables

Writing about exports

A   Use the information in the statistical tables on page 87 to write a short factual passage. The questions on the left will help you to complete the skeleton sentences below.

1st paragraph
What do the figures over the last 20–30 years show?
What has there been, on the one hand?
What has, in addition, almost disappeared?
What can one say, in general, has happened since 1960?

2nd paragraph
What does a detailed examination of the figures do?
What contribution did major crops make in 1960?
What was this reduced to in 1980?
When did the biggest fall come?
What drop did this represent?
Over how many years?
How did the contribution go after that?

3rd paragraph
What sort of contrast do export volumes present?
What sort of years were there although there was a general decline of 5 leading products?
Which years were they for cocoa?
Which years were they for palm kernels?
What were also substantial in the early seventies?

4th paragraph
What can be said in conclusion?
What declined more rapidly than actual export volume?
What about cocoa exports?
What about their share over the period 1960–80?

Agricultural exports

The figures for _____ an overall decline _____. On the one hand _____ a steady fall _____ of the five leading _____ . In addition, the contribution to _____ in value of eight major products _____. In general, one can say that Nigeria has changed from being _____
_____ .

_____ clarifies _____ happened. In 1960 _____ of exports. In _____ . The biggest _____ between _____ when the share _____ _____ only 30.9%, representing a drop of _____. Thereafter, _____ steadily to 1980.

_____ an interesting contrast to the rather gloomy _____.
Although there was _____ , there were several peak years. For _____ _____ For _____ were peak years. Groundnuts and _____ oil exports were _____ .

So, _____
have declined in volume over the past _____ years. But _____ more rapidly than _____ . For example, _____ in 1980 were _____ they were in _____ , but their ___ _____ 2.2% ___ 22.2%.

B   Organise the list of facts below into an essay plan for an essay about 500 words in length.

List of facts

1   In recent years, there has been insufficient production of groundnuts to feed the local crushing mills.
2   Next year Nigeria expects to import 20,000 tonnes of palm oil.
3   Increased urbanisation has led to a change of tastes:
   – decline in demand for traditional foodstuff
   – increase in demand for importations

– attempts by farmers to respond by growing maize, rice, wheat
   a expensive – irrigation
   b difficult – new crops
   c uncompetitive v. cheaper imports
4 Increased Nigerian domestic consumption
5 Price rises pushed up by neighbouring demand in drought areas
6 Poor performance of major government project RBDA
7 But, agricultural development programmes show signs of being successful in the long run 6% increase
8 Domestic markets: farmers poultry producers doing well
9 Time needed for projects to succeed

C   Use your essay plan and the list of facts to write an explanation of the situation described in **A** and shown in the tables on page 87.

Self-assessment

A   Answer the questions below without looking back at the previous pages:

marks

1 Supply one word for each space:
   a When exports _____ imports there is a trade surplus.
   b A trade deficit gets worse if exports increase _____ while imports increase _____ .
   c The trade gap widened _____ $200 million _____ $450 million.
                                                  (5)

2 List four types of statistical graph. (4)

3 Which type of graph is best for showing overall trends? (1)

4 Which kind of graph is best for showing how spending is distributed between different sectors of the economy? (1)

5 Which type of graph is best for showing differences in total amounts of different sectors? (1)

6 Write down opposites of the following words which you might use when describing graphs:
   a gradual   _____
   b rapid   _____
   c peak   _____
   d fall   _____
   e steady   _____
   f downturn   _____
   g recovery   _____
   h surplus   _____
                                                   (8)

Total (20)

B   Check your answers in the Answer Key and make a note of your score. Make sure you understand your mistakes.

Unit 9

The origins of central banking: The economic background

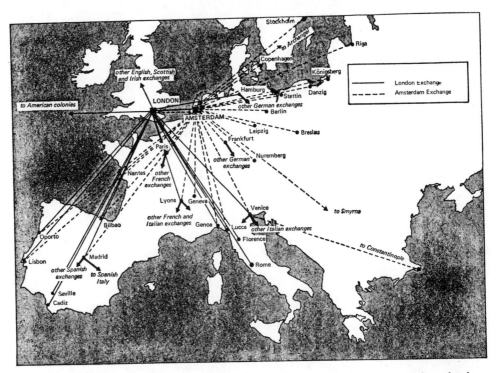

The exchange networks of Amsterdam and London, c. 1700. Amsterdam clearly surpassed London in its range of direct contacts, particularly with Germany and the Baltic

Preview

In this unit you will read about the historical and economic background of the first successful national bank in Europe – the Bank of Amsterdam. You will learn why it was successful and why it was overtaken in importance by the Bank of England. You will also learn

1 to distinguish 16 different forms of money

2 how to write sentences combining clauses which qualify nouns

3 how to write lists of bank services

4 how to use certain phrasal verbs

5 to make notes distinguishing the main point from its supporting evidence

6 to distinguish between main and contributory causes

In the last section you will be able to test your own understanding of what you have done in this unit.

Preparing to read

Survey the SCOPE of the passage
Survey the – Subject
           – Coverage
           – Organisation
           – Purpose of the writer and your own reading purpose
           – Examples of illustrations (in this case the map on page 91)

A   The subject. Think about and discuss the following questions:

1 What is a central bank?
2 What does it do?
3 Is it a private institution or is it government owned?
4 Is the central bank of your country different from that of other countries or is it the same?
5 Can you have an account at your central bank?
6 How does your central bank differ from your ministry of finance or treasury department?
7 Which of these is a central bank?
  a the Bank of America
  b the First National City Bank
  c the Federal Reserve Bank
8 Why are central banks necessary? Illustrate your answer by reference to recent examples of the activities of your central bank.   (London Chamber of Commerce, *Commerce and Finance*, Higher Stage, Spring 1980)
9 What is the difference between a central bank and a commercial bank?   (frequent exam question)

B   Skim the reading passage 'The Economic Background' quickly to understand the coverage.

1 Run your eyes over the passage and look for sums of money, names and dates.

2 Now answer the following:
  a Which century or period of history does the text deal with?
  b Which city's bank does the first part of the text describe?
  c What was the total value of Bank of England notes in 1698?
  d Name three countries mentioned besides England.

3 Quickly read the first line or two of each paragraph.

4 Now write answers to the following:
  a What was the position of Amsterdam in the 17th century?
  b What was the bank at Amsterdam called?
  c What was Amsterdam's position based on?
  d When was the Bank of England founded?

C   Textual organisation. The text is an extract from a longer one.

1 What is the larger text about?
2 What sub-divisions of the larger text does this passage deal with?
3 What is the relationship of the last paragraph to the other four paragraphs?

D The purpose of writer and reader
1 Which of the following best describe the overall purpose of the writer?
historical reporting? narration? argument? persuasion? interpretation? statement of facts? generalisation about events?

2 Look again at the list of reading purposes on pages 64–5 and decide which purpose you might have in reading a text like 'The origins of central banking: the economic background'.

E Examples of illustrations: study the map on page 91 and answer the following:

1 What do you think an *exchange network* is?
2 What is the author's purpose in including the map along with the text? (The passage comes from 'The Emergence of Modern Finance in Europe' by Geoffrey Parker, in the *Fontana Economic History of Europe 1500–1730*, Vol. 2, 1974.)
3 Which parts of Europe did Amsterdam have connections with, which London had no direct connections with?
4 Did London have connections with any parts of the world which Amsterdam did not have connections with?

The passage *The economic background*

A You have already skimmed the passage for the gist. Read it again quickly in the same way, but glancing at every line.

B After a second careful reading, answer the questions on the left.

Numbers refer to lines in the passage.

1 Look forward in the text for the meaning of *Wisselbank* (3).

2 Why *sure*? (3)

3 *the Amsterdam corporation* (5) = local government? national government? public company?

4 Which countries are these cities in? (8–9)

5 *this*, *these* or *those* (12)?

6 *it*, *they* or *she* (13)?

7 Which word (15) means *no one could argue against it*?

8 Find an equivalent phrase for *multilateral payments system* (16) in the first sentence of this paragraph.

The Emergence of Modern Finance in Europe 1500–1730

(*cont. from previous page*)
. . .total issue of deposit certificates never exceeded the total bullion held in the bank).

The Wisselbank thus proved a sure deposit for the working capital of the business community (guaranteed by
5 the Amsterdam corporation) and an efficient clearing-house for credit notes (a free service until 1683). Other exchange banks of the Amsterdam model quickly followed –in Middelburg (1616), Hamburg (1619), Nuremberg and Delft (1621), Rotterdam (1635) and Stockholm (1656)–
10 until in 1697 it was estimated that 25 public banks of one sort or another were in existence in Europe. However, few of _____ later creations could match the power and wealth of the Amsterdam bank; in 1721 _____ had 2,918 accounts worth a total of 28,886,000 florins. From 1660
15 until 1710 at least it was the undisputed capital of European trade, the centre of the first multilateral payments system in the world.

9 *ascendancy* (18) = efficiency? power? superiority?

ubiquity (19) = being everywhere.

10 *maritime* (22): why not *seaside*? why not *coastal*?

11 Supply one word before *meant* (23).

12 *bill of exchange* (25) = foreign currency? credit instrument? receipt for goods?

13 *honoured* (26) = paid? praised? respected?

14 What sort of *bills* (28)?

15 Where were these bills to be paid?

16 Which two words make Amsterdam seem like a fortress?

17 Supply one word for the blank (34).

18 What fish does *tentacles* (34) refer to? (see map)

19 Find a synonym for *supremacy* (36) in the previous paragraph. (18)

20 *show* or *shows* (39)?

21 What sort of *contacts* (40)?

22 Supply one word (40).

23 Which particular *financial service* has already been mentioned?

24 Supply words to complete (42, 43).

25 Which words mean *offset*?

26 *her own network* (42–3) is in contrast with what other network?

27 Supply one word (48).

28 *As Amsterdam's* (51) what?

29 What *prosperity* (52)?

30 Did the Bank of England follow the Amsterdam model?

31 Supply one word (56).

32 Why should the government have to *transfer money overseas* (58)?

at par (59) = at their face value

33 Which words show that the amount of notes had been increasing all the time?

The secret of Amsterdam's financial ascendancy lay in the ubiquity of Dutch trading concerns. Dutch merchants,
20 Dutch shipping and Dutch investment had acquired a foothold in every major commercial centre of Europe, and in most maritime cities of Asia, America and Africa besides, by 1660. _____ meant that Amsterdam was in direct trading contact with virtually every other centre, and
25 that it was possible to buy a bill of exchange in Amsterdam which would be honoured almost anywhere in the world. Some trading areas–the Baltic for instance–would only accept bills drawn on Amsterdam. The city's wide commercial contacts and the great influx of bullion and coin
30 from all corners of the globe (Amsterdam was the European capital of the trade in precious metals too) created very stable exchange rates which further consolidated its commanding trading position. Figure 1 illustrates the extent to which Amsterdam had spread _____ tentacles
35 over Europe by the first decade of the eighteenth century.

Amsterdam's supremacy was only eroded and undermined when the trading contacts and the wealth of the London merchants finally overtook those of Holland. Already in the 1700s, as Figure 1 _____ , London's direct
40 contacts _____ numerous, although during the wars against Louis XIV England was clearly dependent on the financial services of Amsterdam in order to set _____ heavy spending on Marlborough's army against _____ favourable trade balance with France, Holland and Ger-
45 many. It was chiefly after 1713 that Britain expanded her business contacts, profiting from the exotic commodities which poured in from the New World to establish her own network for distributing _____ to the rest of Europe. Based soundly on her expanding trade, Britain built up
50 exchange dealings which were as extensive and as far-flung as Amsterdam's.

At the centre of the new prosperity and supremacy was the Bank of England, founded as a joint-stock company in London in 1694. At first the Bank was intended only to
55 handle a government loan and issue banknotes (known as 'running cash notes') but _____ soon did much else besides: accepting deposits, trading in bullion (like the Amsterdam Wisselbank), transferring money overseas for the government, accepting state securities at par as de-
60 posits or for cash payment, handling tax-revenues for the government, accepting and crediting bills of exchange payable to customers . . . By 1698 the Bank had notes in circulation payable on demand worth £1,340,000. By 1720

34 *paper credits* (67) means what?

35 What were the *innovations* (69–70)?

36 *equivalent* (71–2) to what?

37 Why *specie* (75) deposit notes?

38 In what way was this a disadvantage?

39 *was* or *were* (76)?

40 *foundered* (79) = were successful? started? sank?

41 What is the *early modern period* (82)?

42 *took hold* (82) = grasped? became established? were popular?

43 *English colonies* (85) where?

44 Were the notes accepted at all?

45 *its* or *their* (87)?

65 this total had risen to £2,480,000 (smallest denomination £10) and many other banks in England and Scotland also issued their own notes. In all it was estimated that the total value of paper credits circulating in early eighteenth-century England was about £15,000,000, as against a total coin and bullion stock of £12,000,000. The financial inno-

70 vations of the later seventeenth century had thus expanded England's total monetary stock by 25% without an equivalent increase in the amount of actual currency.

This achievement was impressive but it was also unique. No other European country managed to create money in

75 this way. The highly valued specie deposit notes of the Amsterdam bank _____ never allowed to exceed the total of the deposits until 1781; the brief experiments of a paper currency in Sweden (1661–4) and France (1718–20) quickly foundered because notes exceeded cash reserves

80 by too large a margin and could not be redeemed immediately for coin at par. Apart from England and Scotland, banknotes only took hold in the early modern period in North America, where the government of Canada issued 'playing card' notes after the 1670s and a number of

85 English colonies put 'bills of publick credit' into circulation after 1690–and even then the notes were soon over-issued and ceased to be accepted at _____ face-value. The 'financial revolution' still had its limits.

Ask and answer

A   Ask and answer questions with your colleagues using the tables below:

What	was were is	the Wisselbank a gyrobank the value of the Wisselbank's accounts in 1770 the secret of Amsterdam's financial success running cash notes the difference between the total monetary stock and the total coin and bullion in Britain in the early eighteenth century the exchange contacts of Amsterdam the limitations of the financial revolution	?
What services		did the Wisselbank provide did the Bank of England provide were urgently needed by the governments of the seventeenth century	?

		other banks set up on the Amsterdam model	
Why	were was did	Amsterdam's position so strong economically	?
		the British need the services of Amsterdam in the beginning of the eighteenth century	
		the experiments with paper currency in Sweden and France fail	
		the financial revolution have its limitations	
		the Bills of Publick Credit cease to be accepted at face value	

Any other reason?

B Ask and answer other questions of your own. If you are doubtful about the answers, or the form of the answers, check with your teacher.

Analysis

Word study

Aspects of money We have come across some twenty different expressions which refer to money. These are not synonyms but words for different aspects of money and must be understood in the context in which they are used.

Match the various sorts of money listed on the left with their explanations given in random order on the right. (The left-hand column is divided into categories and the line numbers are shown to help you locate the context in the reading passage.)

Trade and Industry
1 investment (20)
2 working capital (4)
3 credit notes (6)
4 paper credits (67)
5 Bill of Exchange (25)

The government
6 revenues (60)
7 government loans (55)
8 state securities (59)

The banking system
9 total bullion (2)
10 deposit (3)
11 cash reserves (79)
12 multilateral payments (16)

The country as a whole
13 actual currency (72)
14 total monetary stock (71)
15 specie deposit notes (75)
16 deposit certificates (1)

a   a place for keeping money
b   credit instrument
c   bank's receipt for money deposited in it
d   money lent for a commercial enterprise
e   coins held as a stockpile
f   banknotes representing gold or silver in banks
g   money used to buy labour materials or stock-in-trade
h   proceeds of taxation
i   money for a war or other state expenditure
j   certificates representing money lent to the state
k   coins
l   the gold and silver held by a bank
m   an accumulation of cheques and Bills to be settled
n   the whole money supply
o   all types of cheques, bills and promissory notes
p   all types of banknotes, bills, cheques and other money (but not coin)

Combining sentences

A Look at the way these pairs of sentences can be combined:

1 The Wisselbank deposit was a safe place to keep money.
The deposit was guaranteed by the Amsterdam municipality.
  The Wisselbank deposit, guaranteed by the Amsterdam municipality, *was* a safe place to keep money.

2 Britain built up exchange dealings which were as extensive as Amsterdam's.
The exchange dealings were based soundly on her expanding trade.
  Britain *built up* exchange dealings, based soundly on her expanding trade, which were as extensive as Amsterdam's.

3 The Letter of Credit is now available by documents against payment.
The Letter of Credit is confirmed by the advising bank.
  The Letter of Credit, confirmed by the advising bank, *is* now available by documents against payment.

B Note the positions of the main verbs (italicised). Note also the commas. Combine the following pairs of sentences in the same way, but use commas only when necessary to make the meaning clear:

1 The Bank of England was at the centre of the new found prosperity.
The Bank of England was founded as a joint-stock company in 1694.

2 At first the Bank only issued notes but later it went on to provide a great many other services to the government.
The notes were known as 'running cash notes'.

3 The innovations enabled the money supply to be increased by 25% without increasing the amount of metal cash.
The innovations were introduced at the end of the seventeenth century.

4 Experiments with paper currency foundered because notes exceeded gold by too large a margin.
The experiments with paper currency were promoted in Sweden and France.

5 The cheque got lost in the post and so it had to be cancelled.
The cheque was signed by the managing director.

6 To avoid delay, shipping documents should be forwarded to the bank as soon as possible.
The documents should be made out exactly as stated in the credit.

7 Cheques should be made payable to Universal Stores Ltd.
Cheques should be supported by bank cards.

8 Recently the practice of returning cheques with monthly statements was discontinued by many banks.
The cheques were drawn by account holders.

Listing

A Look at the passage (lines 57–62) and note how the activities of the Bank of England at the end of the seventeenth century are listed, using commas.

B   Write a sentence which incorporates the following list of bank services in the same way. Use the verbs given, and begin: *The clearing banks* . . .

current and deposit accounts   standing order payments
credit transfers   travellers' cheques
regular statements   foreign currency

carry out, provide, make, run, change, make available

Phrasal verbs

A   Look at the following example of the use of a phrasal verb:

The solution to the problem, according to monetarist theory *lies in* restricting the money supply.(18)

B   Use a phrasal verb from the passage to complete the following sentences. Line numbers are given to help you find suitable verbs, but be sure to use them in the correct form:

1 Should we accept this cheque _____ _____ an unknown bank? (25–28)

2 One is allowed to _____ _____ normal business expenses _____ taxation. (40–45)

3 Banks, more than anyone else _____ _____ the period of high interest rates. (45–48)

4 The interest charged by the banks for overdrafts is _____ _____ that of the central bank. (48–51)

5 The Arab banks have _____ their activities in the Third World _____ a substantial amount. (69–72)

6 A government permit is needed _____ _____ _____ gold. (55–60)

7 Treasury stock is _____ _____ face value for repayment on their redemption dates. (55–60)

8 The financial futures market _____ _____ _____ as a means of stabilising foreign exchange rates and providing profitable business. (49–51)

9 The company experienced temporary difficulties when receipts were _____ _____ payments for a period. (77–81)

10 On their redemption date the stock will be _____ _____ par. (77–81)

Extension

Generalisation

A Generalisation and evidence (judgement and fact) Study the ways in which information is presented in the first complete paragraph of the passage. Numbers in brackets refer to lines in the passage.

Generalisation	The Wisselbank was a safe place to deposit money (3–4)
Evidence	– guaranteed by Amsterdam corporation (4–5)
Evidence	– 2,918 accounts (13)
Evidence	– 28.8 million florins of liabilities (14)
Evidence	– deposit notes never exceeded total bullion (75–77)
Evidence	– copied by other cities (7–9)
Generalisation	An efficient clearing house (5 and 16)
Evidence	– nil
First generalisation repeated	Undisputed capital of the European trade, centre of first multilateral payments system in the world (15–17)

B Write down the main generalisations of each of the remaining paragraphs. Note down at least three pieces of supporting evidence for each generalisation given by the author.

Main and contributory factors

Decide which alternative is the effective cause or main reason. The other points are contributory factors or untrue.

1 The main reason for the security for depositors of the Wisselbank was:
  a It had 2,918 accounts.
  b Its issue of deposit certificates never exceeded its bullion.
  c It had deposits worth 28,886,000 florins.

2 The other national banking schemes failed because:
  a They could not match the power and wealth of Amsterdam.
  b Dutch trading contacts were everywhere.
  c The amount of their note issues was too great compared with their reserves.

3 The main reason for Amsterdam's financial supremacy until the 1700s was:
  a The influx of bullion.
  b The stability of exchange rates.
  c Its central role in world trade.

4 London superseded Amsterdam because:
  a It became the distribution centre for commodities.
  b Its trading contacts became more numerous.
  c The Bank of England was at its centre.

5 The English banking system prospered because:
  a Its financial innovations enabled it to create money without overissuing notes.
  b The Bank of England supervised the other banks.
  c Most English banks were not simply deposit banks but banks of issue.

Self-assessment

A   Answer the following questions below without looking back at the previous pages:

marks

1 The main difference between the Wisselbank and the Bank of England was that
   a The Wisselbank was richer and had more exchange contacts.
   b The Bank of England issued notes to a greater value than the gold it had on deposit.
   c The Wisselbank had more contacts on the continent of Europe.
   d The Bank of England provided more different kinds of services for the government.   (1)

2 **a** What is skimming?   (2)
   b Why is it advisable to skim a text before reading it in detail?   (2)
   c What sort of information can one find most easily and quickly by skimming?   (3)

3 Multilateral payments system means
   a cheque clearing
   b settling all one's debts
   c paying for international trade   (1)

4 Give a two-word definition of *Bill of Exchange*.   (2)

5 In the passage in this unit, *actual currency* means
   a banknotes
   b gold or silver coins
   c gold or silver bullion
   d all types of money   (1)

6 Rewrite the following two sentences as one sentence:
   The company has already gone bankrupt.
   The company was set up last year.   (4)

7 Complete the following sentence:
   Some bank loans are _____ _____ the principle of joint venture risk.   (2)

8 Generalisations in explanatory texts are normally followed by supporting _____ .   (2)

Total (20)

B   Check your answers in the Answer Key. Make sure you understand your mistakes, if any.

Unit 10

The origins of central banking: the political background

The first Bank of Amsterdam occupied ground-floor rooms (behind the closed door on the right) in this old town hall until the building was burnt down in 1652.

Preview

This unit is concerned with the political background to the financial revolution of the seventeenth and eighteenth centuries. It will also give practice in the following skills:

1 scanning texts to look for specific information

2 asking and answering questions on the same topic but using different forms of question

3 understanding the difference between directly stated and implied information

4 understanding more about sentence structure and certain types of clause

5 practising specialised expressions used in banking and finance

6 note-making

Preparing to read

Surveying before reading

Survey the SCOPE of the text on pages 102–4, 'The Political Background':

A Subject The passage in this unit comes from the same article as the last passage: 'The Emergence of Modern Finance in Europe', by Geoffrey Parker (from *Fontana Economic History of Europe, 1500–1730*, Vol. 2, 1974). You should therefore be able to answer the questions that follow:

1 In what period of history did the events take place?
2 Where was the first international exchange and which countries did it cover?
3 What were the economic conditions which gave rise to the first national banks?
4 Why did the Bank of England survive while other banks failed?

B   Coverage   To get an idea of what the passage is about, skim it for:

1 the information contained in the first two lines of each paragraph
2 some events and dates
3 some sums of money

C   Organisation   Survey the organisation of the text so as to build a framework for note-making. What sort of organisation did the last reading passage have? (Look again at **A** on page 99.) Does 'The Political Background' in this unit have the same pattern?

D   Your reading Purpose   Look again at the reasons for reading listed on pages 63–4. Having a specific reason for reading makes it easier and quicker to read. Think about the following questions. Make it your purpose to look for answers to them in the text:

1 How did events help the setting up of the Bank of England?
2 What caused the decline of the Wisselbank?
3 Why did the Bank of England survive while so many other similar banks failed?

E   Examples of illustrations   The engraving at the head of this unit was taken from another text.

1 What can you tell about the Bank of Amsterdam (Wisselbank) from the picture? Remember that it was perhaps the foremost bank of the world at the time the engraving was made. It was also well established.
2 Why was the bank situated in the Town Hall buildings?

The passage   *The political background*

1 Who was Charles II?

2 *Hardly more successful* (1) than whom? (see next sentence)

3 *predecessors* (2) = officials? bankers? rulers who came before?

4 What was *the right direction* (4)?

practice (5): see p. 67, **E e**

excise (6) = internal tax on tobacco, alcohol etc.

5 *promising* (7) to do what?

Follow the same procedure as in previous units.

Financially speaking, Charles II was hardly more successful. His budgets, like those of his predecessors, were always in deficit; but there were some constructive attempts
to find a solution. A step in the right direction was to aban-
5   don the practice of farming the major taxes: direct collection of the customs was resumed in 1671, of the excise in
1683, of the hearth tax in 1684. More promising still, in
1665 a new instrument of credit was introduced: the 'orders
of payment', issued by government departments to their

6 *constituted* (10) = were? broke? discussed?

7 *Treasury* (11) = Ministry of _____?

8 *accrued* (12) = current? maximum? accumulated?

endorsement (13) = signing on the back (Latin: *in* + *dorsum* = back)

9 Why should we expect a Dutch scheme to be a big improvement?

10 *City* (20) of _____?

11 Which word shows that the holders were angry?

12 *The only solution* (24) to what?

13 Find a synonym for *suspend* (24). (28)

moratorium (26–7) = delay

14 Only *repayable* (27) from _____ taxes.

15 *Orders* (29) of what? (see line 8)

16 What had *serious consequences* (30)?

17 *frozen credits* (31–2) = _____?

18 *conversion* (36) = refusal? abolition? alteration?

19 *principal* (41) = original capital? chief banker? ideal amount?

20 Which words point to the insecurity of public finance?

The new king was Dutch.

21 Who was a predecessor of William?

22 *coherent* (49) = _____? (see *adherent*, *inherent*)

23 *ministers* (50) = Christian priests? royal servants? members of the government?

maladroit (50) = clumsy, unskilful

24 Whose ministers?

the war (53) (see p. 94 l. 41) with France.

25 *spread* (54) over what?

26 *expedients* (55) = helpful loans? convenient methods? successful taxes?

10 creditors in place of cash. The orders constituted a promise by the Treasury to pay a certain sum at a certain date, together (in many cases) with accrued interest. It was possible to assign the orders to a third party (by endorsement) and they were therefore accepted as deposits and payments

15 by the London goldsmith bankers. This scheme, the brainchild of Sir George Downing (Secretary to the Treasury and former ambassador in Holland), was based on a technique of public finance perfected by the Dutch. It was perfectly sound in intention. Trouble only arose at the end of

20 1671 when there was a panic in the City and all those who held orders of payment seethed around the Treasury demanding immediate reimbursement in cash. The total sum involved was £2,250,000 and the government could not pay. The only solution was to suspend payments (as the

25 goldsmiths themselves had done during the 'run' of 1667) and so, on 18 December 1671, the king decreed a moratorium on all the orders not specifically repayable from a fixed future revenue. This move, known as the 'Stop of the Exchequer', affected orders worth about £1,300,000 and it

30 had particularly serious consequences for the handful of leading goldsmith bankers who held almost all the frozen credits. Some of them failed in consequence. Only in 1677 did the bankers reach an agreement with the king by which, although their capital remained frozen, interest of 6 per

35 cent was paid on it.

This clumsy and forcible debt conversion did little to improve the crown's credit. After Charles II's death in 1685 interest payments were suspended and the debt was only recognised again in 1705 (when the government prom-

40 ised to pay interest of 3 per cent 'for ever'; even then the principal was never returned). This was a poor precedent for building up a national debt, yet the war which began with France in 1689 made it necessary to borrow large sums to pay the forces overseas. It became desperately import-

45 ant to set public finance on a surer footing.

Even under William III/progress towards the 'financial revolution'/was surprisingly slow./The king was often absent/and, despite his knowledge of Dutch techniques of debt management,/he provided little coherent advice./In

50 addition,/his ministers were maladroit and inexperienced/, while the House of Commons/had an excessive mistrust of the new ministry/and of any financial innovation./Everyone refused to recognise/that the war would be long and expensive/and that its cost would have to be spread./King

55 William's war/was therefore financed by expedients/not unlike those of the 1650s./Taxation was increased as much

27 *proceeds were anticipated* (57)
= the government spent the
_____ before?/after? they
received it

28 Would a *'perpetual' loan*
(61–2) be repaid?

29 *annuities* (63) = _____ ?
(see *annual* and *securities*)

30 *Annual payments* (64) of
what?

31 *yield* (64) = surrender value?
collection amount? money
product?

32 What does *subscription* (65)
refer to? (see *sub* = under,
scribe = write)

33 *principle* (68) = capital? fact?
idea?

34 Who were the *subscribers*
(74)?
a people who paid interest?
b people who provided the
capital?
c government ministers?

35 *constituted* (78) (note different
meaning from the word on
l. 10) = set up? built?
opened?

36 In Britain the minister of
finance is the Chancellor of
the _____ ?

carried . . . through (88) =
helped to survive financially

as possible/and the proceeds were anticipated by short-term loans./Between 1689 and 1702,/government expenditure totalled £72 million,/of which £63 million came from
60 taxation and anticipations/and only £7 million/–under 10%–/from long-term loans. / The first of these 'perpetual' loans was floated in January 1693 guaranteed by Parliament: £1,000,000 was to be raised by selling life annuities, the annual payments secured on the yield of certain excise
65 duties for the next 99 years. The subscription did not go well (the million had still not been collected a year later) but the life annuity fund of 1693 did set a crucial precedent. It introduced for the first time the principle of government long-term borrowing into England. Parliament at last
70 recognised that the loan was going to be prolonged (it was called 'a Fund of Perpetual Interest') and further long-term loans followed in 1694. In March a lottery was launched to raise £1,000,000 and in April a loan of £1,200,000 was invited at 8%, the subscribers to become incorporated as a
75 joint-stock company entitled 'The Governor and Company of the Banke of England'. This proved to be a great success. The loan was fully subscribed within 11 days and the newly constituted bank went on to raise more loans for the government over and above its original sum. The Bank
80 also agreed to redeem all Exchequer tallies (orders for payment of government debt) presented to it, and it allowed the Treasury to issue the Bank's own 'sealed bills' (promissory notes) to pay its debts. After 1697 the Bank also accepted government credit notes as deposits and as
85 subscriptions to new public loans (an operation which almost ruined the Bank but saved the government's credit). The Bank of England's activity as an agent for raising long-term loans carried the ministers of William III through to the Peace of Rijswijk in September 1697.

Discussion

Ask and answer

Practise asking and answering the questions below. They are *examples* of questions you might use. There are follow-up questions shown in brackets. Use these if you are not satisfied with the answers.

Paragraph 1

1 What sort of problems did Charles II and his government have?
steps were taken to solve them?
(How did they try to solve them?)
(What else did they do?)
measures were more successful than others in dealing with the problems?

2 What problems did Charles II and his government have?
        steps were taken to overcome them?
        (How did they try to solve them?)
        (Which of these steps was the most promising?)
        else did they do?
        measures proved the most successful?
        advantages did the 'orders of payment' have?
        (What else could they do with them?)
        problems arose from them?
        (Anything else?)
        sum was involved?
        (How much did the government owe?)
        solution did the government adopt?
        agreement did the bankers reach with the king?

3 What was/were the hearth tax?
        (What do you mean?)
        tax farming?
        the 'orders of payment'?
        (How did they work?)
        the Stop of the Exchequer?
        (Why was it necessary?)

4 Why did Charles II have financial problems?
        his government abandon the practice of tax-farming?
        the government suspend payments of the 'orders of
          payment'?
        the Stop of the Exchequer have serious consequences for
          some of the leading goldsmiths?

5 Why were Charles II's budgets always in deficit?
        (Could you clarify that?)
        (You mean to say that he was bankrupt?)
  was the practice of tax farming abandoned?
        a new instrument of credit introduced in 1665?
        (What do you mean?)

B Now ask and answer similar questions about the rest of the passage. Don't forget the follow-up questions.

Sense groups

Any written text can be divided into *sense groups*, i.e. groups of words that seem to belong together and together have meaning.

A Study the section (ll. 46–61) of the passage which has been divided into sense groups. This is to help you understand the structure of the sentences. Read it aloud, or listen to it being read, with a pause at each mark.

B Continue to the end of the passage, marking it into sense groups in the same way. There is no hard-and-fast rule about it. Group together the words which seem to you to make sense or sound right together. Compare your results with those of other students, or check them with your teacher.

Analysis

Statement and implication

A Study the statements from the text on the left and the meaning implied by the writer on the right. The numbers in brackets refer to lines in the passage.

Statement	**Implication**
The writer writes . . .	The writer implies . . .
A step in the right direction was to abandon the practice of farming the major taxes. (4)	The practice of farming major taxes was a bad one.
It was perfectly *sound in intention.* (19)	In actual practice it did not work.
Only in 1677 did the bankers reach an agreement with the king . . . (32)	It took a long time for the bankers to get any concessions from the king.
This clumsy and forcible debt conversion *did little to improve* the crown's credit. (36)	In fact, it did a lot to destroy the government's credit.

NOTE   The implication is shown mostly by the words in italics.

B In the remaining examples, underline those words on the left which imply the meaning given on the right:

1 . . . the debt was only recognised again in 1705 . . . (38)	It was a very long time before the claims of the government's creditors were recognised.
2 Everyone refused to recognise that the war would be long and expensive . . . (52)	It was obvious that the war would be long and expensive.
3 . . . only £7 million – under 10% – came from long-term, loans. (60)	£7 million was a very small proportion of the cost of the war to be financed by government borrowing.
4 . . . further long-term loans followed in 1694. In March a lottery was launched . . . and in April a loan of £1,200,000 was invited at 8% . . . (71)	Setting up the Bank of England was just another among many schemes for raising money for the government.
5 The Bank of England's activity as an agent for raising long-term loans carried the ministers of William III through to . . . (87)	The government was virtually dependent on the Bank of England.

Writing sentences

A Look at the following sentence:
Direct collection of customs was resumed.
Writers give prominence to something by putting it at the beginning of the sentence. Study how you can change a sentence to do this. The emphasised items are in italics in the first two examples:

The Secretary to the Treasury introduced a new instrument of credit.
A new instrument of credit was introduced by the Secretary to the Treasury.

Government departments issued the 'orders of payment'.
The 'orders of payment' were issued by government departments.

The goldsmiths accepted the orders as deposits and payments.
The orders were accepted as deposits and payments by the goldsmiths.

They increased taxation as much as possible.
Taxation was increased as much as possible.

NOTE   *by them* would be clumsy and is usually omitted.

B   Make sure, when you write sentences like this, that you use the forms was/were and get the past participle of the verb correct. Rewrite the following in the same way to emphasise the prominent item:

1 They anticipated the proceeds of taxation by long-term loans.

2 Long-term loans financed only 10% of the cost of the war.

3 Parliament guaranteed the first of these 'perpetual' loans, which was floated in 1693.

4 The life annuity fund of 1693 introduced for the first time the principle of government long-term borrowing.

5 The city raised £1,000,000 though a lottery in March.

6 Then in April they invited a loan of £1.2 million.

7 The government suspended interest payments in 1685 and only recognised the debt in 1707.

8 Last year the National Bank opened several branches in the country.

9 The IMF approved a large loan for the government on condition that taxation was increased.

10 The Chancellor announced massive cutbacks in government spending.

C   Look at the following sentence:
Understandably, he was very annoyed.

Now study these examples from the text:

Financially speaking, Charles II was . . . (1)

More promising still, in 1665 a new instrument of credit was introduced . . . (7)

. . . progress towards the financial revolution was *surprisingly* slow. (46)

Notice the alternative position of the adverb phrase – after the verb. The words in italics express the writer's comment on what he is saying and could be replaced as follows:

1 *From the financial point of view* . . .

2 *I think that it was more promising that* . . .

3 *It seems surprising to us that* . . .

D   Now write your own examples by joining up the phrases on the left with suitable sentences from the right-hand column:

1 Understandably
2 Undeniably
3 Happily
4 Not surprisingly
5 Without the slightest doubt

a the robbery last night was carried out by terrorists.
b the bank was unable to cash his cheque.
c the bank was able to cash his cheque.
d the security guard was a very brave man.
e he was very shocked when he looked at his bank statement.

E Now write sentences of your own on banking topics, using the following expressions. (Punctuate them correctly, as in the examples, using capital letters and commas.)

1 without wishing to exaggerate
2 on the positive side
3 even more important
4 from the account-holder's point of view

F Look at the following sentence:
Robert Macnamara, president of the world bank, . . .

Study the grammatical structure of the following examples:

1 Mr Williams, the manager of my bank, . . .

2 Francois Mitterand, the French prime minister, . . .

3 . . . a new instrument of credit was introduced: the 'orders of payment', . . . (8)

4 This scheme, the brain-child of Sir George Downing, was based on . . . (15)

5 . . . Sir George Downing, Secretary to the Treasury and former ambassador in Holland, . . . (16)

This style of writing is quite common in bank reports and newspapers:

6 The Ministry of Energy and a Canadian firm, Levali International, have signed an agreement . . .

7 Mr Yasuhiro Nakasone, previously head of the Administrative Management Agency, was elected . . .

8 . . . the move was endorsed by the Chartered Bank, the other note-issuing bank in Hong Kong.

G Now write your own examples by completing the following so that they make sense for a country you know. Use as many words as you need:

1 . . ., the mainstay of the economy, was given an additional boost by the minister's announcement.

2 Mr . . ., the leader of the . . ., gave details of the government's spending cuts.

3 The . . ., funded by the . . ., was granted a low interest loan of $. . .

4 Mr . . ., the governor of the Central Bank, announced . . . in interest rates.

Complex sentences

In Units 2 (p. 25) and 7 (pp. 75–6) you practised analysing complex sentences. In this unit you have practised dividing complex sentences into their sense groups. All these activities help to make you more aware of sentence structure. The groups of clauses below have been taken from good sentences and put into random order. Rewrite them in the correct order, with punctuation, so that they make sense:

1 Economic Bulletin
continued to be dampened
according to Bank Negara's latest quarterly
economic activity in the second quarter of 1982
by the prolonged recession

2 reflecting weak international demand for primary commodities
gross export earnings
at the level of the corresponding quarter of 1981
stagnated

3 declined
except for palm oil and palm kernels
production of other major commodities

4 remained relatively strong
while manufacturing output recovered moderately
mining production
due to increased oil production

5 aggregate domestic demand in the second quarter
was generally sustained
and a sharp rise in public sector spending
by continued moderate growth in private sector expenditure

6 although this was slower than the 32.4% growth in the corresponding
quarter of 1981
imports of consumer goods
at an annual rate of 11.5%
continued to increase

Extension

Phrasal verbs   **A**   Make as many sentences as you can from the tables:

1	The central bank provides	the government	*with*	finance.
		finance	*for*	the government.

2	The company	repaid / paid	their creditors / their debts / their old employees / their workers	*in*	cash. silver. gold. oil.
				by	cheque. credit note. Bill of Exchange. promissory note.
				with	gratitude. dismissal. a golden handshake. redundancy. pleasure. wage increases.

| 3 | They raised | a loan
finance
money | *from* the bank *for* the project.
in the market. |

B   Check your sentences with your teacher or fellow students.

Note-making

A   Read section **C** (page 102) on **Organisation** again and then study the notes below:

A.   Weak finances of Charles II   Deficit budgeting

B.   Attempted solutions, constructive
1.   tax farming ended
2.   direct taxation resumed
   – customs   1671
   – excise   1683
   – hearth tax   1684
3.   Orders of Payment 1665
   – promise to pay + interest
   – could be assigned by endorsement to someone else
     therefore acceptable as payment by goldsmith-bankers

C.   Sound in intention but failed in practice (*positive evaluation with negative implication*)
1.   Panic in the City led to demands for repayment
2.   Government unable to pay
3.   Moratorium declared by the king on £1.3m worth of orders
4.   therefore: bankruptcy of goldsmiths

D.   Agreement with bankers not reached until 1677 (*implied judgement*: it was an unreasonably long time before the matter was partly put right)
1.   capital frozen
2.   but interest 6% paid on it

B   Now continue making notes on the reading passage in the same way.

Formal language in banking

Which synonym? Select the correct word:

1 /Alteration/Change/Modification/Conversion/ of short-term debt into long-term debt is called 'funding'.

2 An important aim of debt /management/control/manipulation/supervision/ is to absorb the total of all debt /certificates/instruments/bills/paper/.

3 During the crisis the US banks in London /delayed/held up/froze/stopped/ all Ruritanian government accounts and subsequently /suspended/refused/delayed/cut/ all interest payments on them.

4 In April the government /set up/floated/inaugurated/initiated/ a new /edition/series/issue/set/ of stock which was quickly /sold out/oversubscribed/mopped up/taken over/ by the market.

5 It is sometimes necessary for the payee to /endorse/countersign/acknowledge/confirm/ a cheque by signing on the back.

6 The government can finance a short-term /squeeze/budget deficit/overspending/shortage of cash/ by long-term borrowing.

Self-assessment

A   Answer the questions below without looking back at the previous pages:

marks

1 How can you best get a rough idea of a passage before reading it in detail? (2)

2 How can you make sure of having a specific reason for reading? (2)

3 Which of the following was the main reason for setting up national loan schemes?
a the need to control government expenditure
b the government need for money
c the slowness of tax-collecting
d the government's desire to end the hearth tax (1)

4 Which of the following was *not* a problem with previous loans like the 'orders of payment'?
a They were too subject to sudden panics.
b They promised payment before the government was in a position to repay.
c They were based on foreign financial techniques.
d There was never enough money to repay them. (1)

5 What was the main difference between the government loan of April 1694 and previous loans?
a It was the first long-term loan.
b It was used to pay for the war.
c The subscribers made themselves into a bank.
d The new bank raised further loans. (1)

6 Complete these phrases:
a the _____ of the exchequer (1)
b the cost had to be _____ over a number of years (1)
c the government's budget was in _____ (1)
d during the take-over negotiations share-dealings in the company were _____ (1)

7 Complete:
Sometimes writers express themselves indirectly. They suggest or _____ things instead of stating them directly. The reader has to understand both the stated facts and the _____ of what he reads. (2)

8 Rewrite the following sentences in the way indicated:
a A new loan was launched a few years later at 7%.
They . . . (2)
b The new bank provided a variety of important services.
A variety . . . (2)
c The bank was in trouble early in January. (clearly) (1)
d Megaprom were appointed by the bank as receiving agents. (Megaprom are well-known import agents)
Megaprom, . . . , were appointed . . . (2)

Total (20)

B   Check your answers in the Answer Key. Make sure you understand your mistakes.

Unit 11

Banking and development:
The role of the traditional sector

Preview

This unit follows on from Unit 6 which was about question analysis, based on the problems of customers using banks. Here you are going to

1 analyse exam questions on development banking

2 look at different ways of planning answers

3 collect information from a text to answer a question

4 identify the main point and supporting detail in a paragraph of deductively arranged material

5 study an inductively organised paragraph

6 make notes

7 identify signpost expressions – words which introduce new sections of the text

8 use your own knowledge of the subject to broaden your understanding of the text

9 practise understanding implication

Preparing to read and write

Essay question 1

A   Writing an essay: Small-scale and cottage industries   Prepare your answer to an essay question step by step, in the same way as you prepare for reading (SCOPE). Survey the subject, decide how much of it you will cover, how you plan to organise your material, what the purpose of your answer is, and what kind of examples you will need to prove your points.

Begin with this question on development banking:

Bring out clearly the role of small-scale and cottage industries in industrialisation. Take your examples from your country. (adapted from *Elements of Economics and Structure of the Indian Economy*, Ref. Code NoH2282, The Institute of Bankers, Bombay)

B   Subject and coverage   What is the question about? (topic analysis)

1 small-scale industries
  – recent role in industrialisation
  – future potential role
2 cottage industries
  – recent role in industrialisation
  – future potential in industrialisation

C   Organisation   You could organise your essay like this:

Paragraph 1	General statement briefly answering the question (see **D** below)			
		examples		
		recent developments	future potential	implications for industrial development
Paragraph 2	small-scale			
Paragraph 3	cottage			
Paragraph 4	Concluding restatement of initial generalisation			

NOTE   This is just one way of organising your answer. You may decide to organise it in a different way. The important point to remember is that, one way or another, *you need to organise your answer to the question clearly*.

D   Purpose Your purpose is to answer the question. For the best effect you should answer it *at the beginning* of your essay.

examples
Small scale and cottage industries are playing an extremely important role in industrialisation, especially in the East.

The role of small scale and cottage industries is of little significance in industrialisation, with the possible exception of the North.

Small scale and cottage industries are a vital component of . . . etc.

E   Using examples Your reading should provide you with examples to illustrate the points you wish to make. These will affect the way you organise your answer. You are told to base your answer on existing examples in your country. Clear and pertinent examples will strengthen and enliven your answer and are worth searching for and noting down as you read.

Essay question 2

A   Writing an essay: Attracting more Customers to the Banks
Write 400–450 words on 'Attracting more Customers to the Banks'.
(from *English*, The Nigerian Institute of Bankers, Part I examinations, 1980)

B   Subject and Coverage (topic analysis)

1 Private account customers: publicity and recruitment methods
  – rural sector
  – urban sector
  (socio-economic groups
  – white collar
  – blue collar etc.)

2 Corporate accounts: publicity and recruitment methods
  Breakdown of likely types of company account:
  – their needs for financial services
  – the media available to bring these to their attention
  – how best to present the banks as providers of services

C   Organisation The topics are distributed into essay paragraphs:

			possible approaches			
Paragraph 1	A general statement answering the question: (see **D** below)					
		summary of banking needs	newspapers	magazines journals	TV	direct approach
Paragraph 2	private customers rural sector					
Paragraph 3	private customers urban sector (by socio-economic groups) a b c					
Paragraph 4	corporate customers type a type b etc					
Paragraph 5	Summary of conclusions and restatement of initial short answer to the question as in paragraph 1 (see examples below).					

D   Writing purpose Be clear about your writing task (See Unit 6, pp. 57–8). Always answer the question briefly in the first paragraph, so that the reader can get an idea of what you mean to say. For example:

> More customers could easily be attracted to the banks by a concerted publicity campaign. The best approach for the country as a whole would be to . . .

> Attracting more customers to the banks is a vital national task.

> Attracting more customers to the banks, while not a national priority at the moment, is an important economic activity.

Your conclusions in the final paragraph will not only summarise what you have said, but will also restate, for the reader's benefit, what you said at the beginning.

Planning answers

A   Practice Draw an essay organisation table for one of the above two questions like the ones under Essay Questions 1 and 2. Organise your paragraphs according to the situation in your own country and the sort of examples you want to use. For instance, you may want to deal with cottage industries or banking publicity by region. You may want to organise your answer by publicity media (for the banking question) or by type of industry (for the cottage industry question).

B   Discussion Here is another way of laying out your organisation structure:

1 Read the question below and study the diagram on page 115:

Discuss the banker's responsibility to society. (Banker's Certificate, Stage 1, Malaysian Institute of Banking, April 1982)

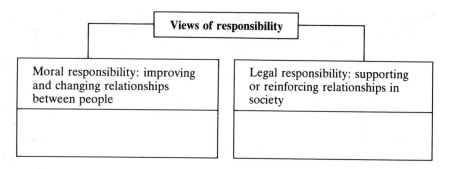

2 Now decide which of the expressions listed below should go in the left box and which should go in the right box of the diagram:

equal opportunities
rules and regulations
national economic development
contracts

fair wages
security of property
labour intensive projects
ownership of property

3 Can you think of any other factors which should be included in the boxes? If so, discuss them with your fellow students before listing them in the diagram.

4 Study the diagram below. How will it affect your answer to the question above? Will you take both sides into account or only one? Which?

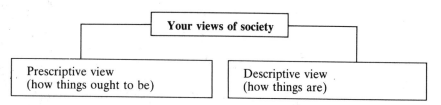

C   Writing purpose If your answer is going to take into account all four views shown in the diagrams in **B** above, it will be an *exposition text*. If your answer takes into account only one, two or three of the views, it will be an *argument text*. Decide which sort of essay you are going to write. But note that *Discuss*, in the question, indicates that you should take into account as many points of view as possible.

D   You may wish to consider a further dimension:

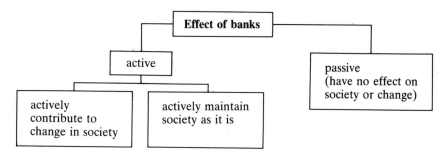

What is your view about the effect of banks? Clarifying your own views will help you to organise an effective answer.

How content of text is organised

A   Study the example below of *inductive* organisation of content. (*inductive* = given certain facts, a general conclusion follows) The notes on the left will help you:

Notes

The topic is clearly introduced.

Particular features are listed.

The generalisation arises out of a summary of the listed features.

The Unorganised Money Market

The unorganised money market can be differentiated from the organised market by the following characteristics:

a Money-lending is often combined with other commercial activities such as trading and manufacturing.
5 b Business is very informal.
c Contact is usually personal.
d The accounting system is fairly simple.
e There is a great deal of flexibility in loan operations.
f Financial transactions are highly secret.

10 Thus, it may be said that it is in the methods rather than in the nature of the business that the unorganised money market differs from the organised market. In contrast to the former, the organised money market is characterised by specialisation, formality, impersonal styles of business
15 dealing, comprehensive accounting systems and lending governed by regulation.

B   Study the example below of *deductive* organisation of content. (*deductive* = given that a general statement is true, certain facts follow):

The writer begins with some general statements

. . . and goes on to support them with detailed instances.

Decline of Indigenous Bankers

There is reason to believe that the decline of business conducted by indigenous bankers has accelerated since
20 independence and since the nationalisation of the 14 major banks.

The State Bank of India, commercial banks and co-operative banks are making heavy inroads into the rural areas previously served only by indigenous bankers. This is
25 partly because of the limited funds at the latters' disposal and their antiquated modes of operation, to which they still cling . . . Only a few of the indigenous bankers have adopted modern methods . . . issuing passbooks, cheque-books, receiving savings deposits and so on.

C   Answer the questions below. Numbers in brackets refer to lines in the text above:

1 *unorganised* (1) = unofficial? disorganised? private?

2 This (5) implies that business in the organised money market is very _____?

3 So, (6) in the organised market business is _____?

4 So (8) you could say of the unorganised market that each loan has a new set of _____ governing it.

5 *Indigenous* (19) = unorganised? home-grown? Indianised?

6 Do lines 18–19 mean
  a there has been less business?
  b there has been more business?
  c business has been faster?

7 We can assume that there are
  a no private banks left.
  b numerous small private banks.
  c only a few private banks left.

8 The main reason for the government-controlled banks taking over business from the private sector is that
  a they are building large roads in the rural areas.
  b they are using modern methods of banking.
  c they are clinging to antiquated methods.

Question analysis and note-making

A Analyse the following questions. (See Unit 6, pp. 57–8 **A** and **C**.)
For each question
– List the topics under which you might begin to make notes.
– Write down appropriate question functions (choose from the list of functions on p. 58 **B**). Be as specific as possible: *review the* _____ , *define what is meant by* _____ , etc:

1 Discuss in brief rural debt and investment in your country. How could the position of farmers be improved through existing credit institutions?

2 Given a multi-agency approach in rural credit, what problems are likely to arise and how could they be solved?

3 To what extent can private sector banking contribute towards development.

4 Why is public sector banking necessary for economic development? What functions, if any, can be left to private and traditional credit agencies?

B Check the functions you have listed against those in the Answer Key. Various answers are possible. The work you have done here will help you when you come to make notes on the Reading passage on banking in India.

The passage *The traditional sector*

A Skim the first lines of each paragraph to get a general idea of what the text is about.

B Read the passage carefully.

C   Answer the questions on the left, which are about vocabulary and details of the text.

NOTE   You may need to use your outside knowledge to answer some of these questions.

The subject of this existential sentence is *a banking system* (2) but prominence is given to *there has existed for an unknown period* . . . (1)

1   *more suitable* (4) than the description _____ _____?

2   What type of commercial organisation does *joint-family* (6) mirror?

3   What part of the *credit requirement* (11) does the forecast not cover?

4   How do *commercial banks* (13) differ from *traditional sector banks* (p. 116 **A**)?

5   *in kind* (24) = in goods? benevolently? to children?

6   What proportion of the true market value would a money-lender pay for a gold bracelet?

7   If this is what the writer says about the indigenous bankers, what does he imply about the money-lenders?

8   The *most important* (40) what?

The Traditional Sector

As in many developing countries, there has existed in India for an unknown period of time a banking system that is called (inaccurately) the 'unorganised sector'. The description 'traditional sector' would be more suitable, as its
5   development goes back in a centuries-old tradition. It is concerned with 'joint-family' enterprises or those based on close personal relationships that can better be described as finance institutions or 'non-banking financial intermediaries' than as banks in the modern sense. Their importance
10   can be seen from the fact that the *All India Credit Review* forecast short- and medium-term credit requirements of Rs 25 billion in 1974, of which only half would come from commercial banks; the balance, inevitably, would come from indigenous sources.
15   The traditional credit sector consists of various small groups which, in different parts of the country, have varied professional designations and are very strongly concentrated in certain trades. Until the middle of the nineteenth century, they even provided the governments of the
20   princely states of the time with loans. These functions were gradually taken over by commercial banks with the support of the colonial government. In general one distinguishes today between:
a the money-lenders–who frequently lend in kind or in
25   very small amounts; they pawn jewellery with a 30–50% margin and lend on a day-to-day basis (for example to the vegetable vendors of Madras); and
b the indigenous bankers.
The second group is distinguished from the first in that the
30   institutions:
a grant no consumer credit;
b accept deposits and thus do not operate only with their own capital (95% of money-lenders do not accept deposits);
35   **c** deal in *hundis*–a kind of promissory note–and thereby have access to the financial market.
Hundis are the credit instruments of the indigenous bankers–promises to pay in writing, in which, although not all the legal features of a promissory note in the sense of the
40   Negotiable Instruments Act 1881 are inherent, the most important ones for lending transactions are present. Up to now there has been no legally valid definition of a *hundi*. Its

9 *current* (44) = flowing? supplied? in use?

usance (50) = time allowed for payment (see *usurious*, p. 71, l. 14)

10 *grace* (54) = permitted delay? mercy? thankfulness?

11 Which type of *hundi* (49) can one infer (from what the writer says) travels furthest?

12 *parties* (58) = celebrations? political groups? people or companies?

13 Which type of *hundi* (50) would be used by someone who wants to be paid cash?

14 What is one way in which a *hundi* differs from a foreign Bill of Exchange?

15 Why should October–April be the *busy season* (65)?

16 *recognised* (68) by whom?

17 *dependent* (72) for what?

18 To what extent is the indigenous sector dependent on the other banks?

19 What does *the first* (78) refer to?

rediscount (81) = buy at a bigger discount than the going market rate (service offered by central banks to alleviate liquidity shortage in the money market)

form is determined by customs and usages and, indeed, the actual wording current in different parts of the country. It
45 serves in general one of several purposes:
a procurement of liquid cash;
b transfer of cash assets;
c financing of inland (domestic) business.
There are two kinds of *hundi*: *dashani* (on sight) and
50 *muddati* (usance). The *dashani* is payable on presentation. It is used only for financing domestic business and in transfers of cash assets by indigenous banks . . .
The *muddati* is payable in general at 90, but also at 30, 60 or 120 days, with usually one to five days' grace. In con-
55 trast with the *dashani*, the *muddati* operates only within local limits–greater significance is attached to the former. Other types of *hundi* are *shah jog* and *nam jog*, which are paid to specified parties, and *dekhaner jog*, effectively a bearer *hundi*. The *jokhim* is similar to a documentary bill
60 of exchange, but is now rare. Externally it cannot be seen from a *hundi* whether the loan presupposes a transaction of goods or whether it deals purely with paper money. If the resources of the banker, of a caste or group, are not sufficient, the *hundi* can be rediscounted by certain com-
65 mercial banks. This refinancing–usually in the busy season (October–April)– is one of the most important points of contact between the organised and unorganised sectors. Indeed, the *hundi* is recognised as a cheap, convenient and efficient way to finance goods; although unsecured and
70 endorsed five times or more, they are rarely dishonoured.
As the credit institutions of the organised sectors are dependent on the Central Bank, a chain can thereby be constructed, which from the Central Bank via the organised banks, the urban indigenous banker and the rural
75 indigenous banker, reaches the smallest money-lender in the villages. It is, however, questionable whether the last link feels anything when the Central Bank operates on the first. The connection, therefore, between the Central Bank and the traditional credit sector comes about only in a
80 roundabout way via a third party, i.e. mostly via the local banker, with whom the Central Bank does not rediscount *hundis*. So, apart from times of general scarcity of credit (July–November) the impact of the measures of the Central Bank is weak in the markets of the unorganised
85 sectors. While money-market rates in recent years have fluctuated greatly, the *hundi* discount rate remained fairly stable (8¾–10½%) until 1973, although since that time, it has risen significantly and is currently in the range of

ceilings (89) = maximum
prices

fiscally (91) = from the tax
point of view

20 Which *measure* (94)?
(The First Banking
Commission Report (94))

14–16%. Some states impose interest-rate ceilings. The
90 *hundi*-business has been hit hard by income tax regulations
(s. 40 (A) (3), Income Tax Act). In order to be fiscally
recognised, all payments over Rs 2,500 must be made by
draft or crossed cheque. The dramatic effect of this
measure on *hundi*-business led the Commission to call for
95 its immediate revocation.

In spite of the differences mentioned, no clear line of
demarcation can be drawn between money-lenders and
indigenous bankers.

D Study the notes beneath, which concern the
overall organisation of the text. As you continue
you will be asked to complete the notes yourself.

Framework for notes
An introductory general statement about
the traditional sector (1–3)
– supporting detail (3–5)
– supporting detail (5–9)

Main point: economic importance of *traditional
sector* (9–14)

Example of notes:
What is the *traditional sector*? (15ff.)
a merchant bankers
– 19th c loans to states taken over by
commercial banks
– trading functions

b money-lenders
– day-to-day loans
– pawnbroking (large discounts)
(definition of *indigenous banks* completed)

Now complete the notes:
What are *hundis*?
Definition (introduced by *Hundis* at the opening
of the paragraph beginning at line 37): _____
a Promises to _____
– although (concession)

b No legal def.

c Purpose 1 _____
2 _____
3 _____

d Types of *hundi* (49ff.)
1 *dashani* – _____
– _____
– _____
2 *muddati* – _____
– _____
3 *shah jog* – _____
4 *nam jog* – _____
5 _____ – _____ etc.

E Then answer these questions on the
organisation of the passage.

1 Main point of section introduced by
Indeed . . . (68) for emphasis. This conclusion
is arrived at after presentation of details.
Is the organisation of the section (53–70)
inductive or *deductive*?

2 What is the main point of lines 71–95?

3 Is the material in this paragraph organised
inductively or deductively?

4 What piece of evidence does the writer give to
support his assertion that the *impact of
measures of the Central Bank is weak in the
markets*? (83–84)

5 Do the last three sentences (89–95) support or
contradict the main point of the paragraph?
Why?

Discussion

Ask and answer

A Ask and answer the following questions:

1 What are the two main types of indigenous financial business which are found today in India?
2 That's one. What was the other one?
3 What central banking function did the traditional banking sector in India once perform?
4 Would it be possible to borrow from a traditional banker to buy a car? Why? Why not?
5 What other instrument of credit is a *hundi* like? How is it different?
6 What can *hundis* be used for? Is there any type of business that they are not used for? Any other type?
7 How does the modern commercial sector help the traditional one?
8 Any other way?
9 What are the main advantages of *hundi* finance?
10 What other advantages are there? Anything else?
11 How is agricultural credit provided in your country?
12 How is the Central Bank in India connected with the village money-lenders?
13 In what ways was *hundi* finance better than normal bank loans during the 1970s?
14 What disadvantages are there in *hundi* finance?
15 Anything else?
16 What comparable traditional credit system exists in your own country? How does it work?
17 How do the traditional bankers in India differ from ordinary modern banks?
18 Any other way?
19 How did the authorities try to collect taxes from the *hundi* dealers recently?
20 Why did the regulation that payments should be made by crossed cheque or draft have a dramatic effect on *hundi* business?

B Ask your own questions and answer questions put by other students.

Analysis

Omitting 'which' and 'that'

A Look at the following:

. . . a banking system called the 'unorganised sector'.

Some sentences can be written without *which* or *that*.

There is a banking system (that is) called the 'unorganised sector'.
There is a banking system called the 'unorganised sector'.

It is concerned with joint-family enterprises (that are) better described as 'non-banking financial intermediaries'.
It is concerned with joint-family enterprises better described as 'non-banking financial intermediaries'.

Notice that using *which* or *that* gives more emphasis:

Other types of *hundi* are the *shah jog* and *nam jog* paid to specified parties.
Other types of *hundi* are the *shah jog* and *nam jog* which are paid to specified parties.

In the following, the *which* cannot be omitted:

The traditional sector consists of various small groups which have varied professional designations.
A chain can be constructed from the Central Bank which reaches the smallest money-lender in the villages.

B Now decide which of the following can be rewritten without *which* and write them out, omitting the *which* as in the first three examples above:

1 The traditional credit sector which is concentrated in certain trades has various professional designations.
2 The traditional sector, which has various professional designations, is concentrated in certain trades.
3 Money-lenders frequently lend on a day-to-day basis against jewellery which is taken at a 30–50% margin.
4 Money-lenders frequently lend against jewellery which is discounted at 50–30% on a day-to-day basis.
5 The indigenous bankers discount *hundis* which are traded in much the same way as Bills of Exchange and operate with their own capital.
6 The indigenous bankers lend money by drawing *hundis* which they buy and sell like Bills of Exchange.
7 The specialised services to agriculture which are provided by the indigenous banking system, could not be easily replaced by the modern banking sector.
8 The *hundi* discount rate, which remained relatively stable during the late sixties, compared favourably with the money market rates in the same period.

Using 'can be . . .ed'

A Look at the following sentence:

They *can be better described* as non-banking financial intermediaries. (7)

Study further examples of this type of sentence:

A chain *can thereby be constructed* from the Central Bank to the money-lender. (72)

It *cannot be seen* from a hundi whether the loan presupposes a transaction of goods or not. (61)

The hundi *can be rediscounted* by certain commercial banks. (64)

B Use the notes to write further examples. Be certain to put the main part of the verb in the correct form. Do not forget the past tense ending:

1 No clear line of demarcation (draw) between money-lenders and indigenous bankers.
2 Whether other business (carry on) with banking activities depends on the social standing of the banker.

3 A substantial amount of business (transact) with a broker who charges a commission.
4 Some people think that the traditional financial services (easily integrate with) the modern sector.

Opening phrase with 'as'

A   Look at the following:

As in many developing countries . . . (1)

This useful opening phrase is used to connect what the reader knows already to what the writer is about to say. It qualifies the main part of the sentence: . . . there has existed in India for an unknown period of time a banking system called the 'unorganised sector'.

Variations you could use are:
As in the examples mentioned above, . . .
As in the case of other large banks, . . .
As can be seen from the evidence, . . .

Do not confuse this type of phrase with *as* meaning *because*:
As the credit institutions of the organised sector are dependent on the Central Bank, . . . (71)

B   Now complete the following:

1 (many other countries) there is a severe unemployment problem
2 (by anyone who examines the facts) it was a clear case of fraud
3 (my bank manager knows) I always repay my loans in good time
4 (undoubtedly the case) in many developing countries internal trade is heavily dependent on traditional finance

Expressing concession

A   Look at the following:

. . . although not all the legal features . . . are inherent, . . . (39)

although expresses concession and works rather like the logical link words studied on page 49. (Study the other examples in the passage on lines 38, 69 and 87.)

There are two other ways of expressing concession in the text:

While money market rates have fluctuated greatly in recent years, . . . (85)
(= Although money market rates have fluctuated . . .)
and
In spite of the differences, . . . (96)
(= Although there are differences . . .)

NOTE   *in spite of* cannot be followed by a verb. But *although* and *while* have to have verbs after them.

B   Now rewrite the sentences below, using *although*, *while* or *in spite of* as indicated:

1 interest rates were high/people still borrowed money (although)
2 high interest rates/the money supply increased as fast as ever (in spite of)
3 there was considerable demand for the new car/sales remained at a low level (while)

4 loans to agriculture were only 3.5% of the total credit/their important role in financing the movement of agricultural produce (in spite of)

5 indigenous bankers tend to be concentrated in urban areas/they fulfil a vital function in areas where commercial banks are unrepresented (although)

Extension

Use of vocabulary

A   Some banking verbs Look at the following:

. . . based on close personal relationships . . .

Study how the following verbs are used in the passage. Line numbers are given in brackets:

List 1
is determined by (43)
is distinguished from (29)
lend on (26)
provided . . . with (19–20)
describe as (7)

List 2
consists of (15)
are concentrated in (17)
deal in (35)
distinguishes between (22)
deals with (62)

List 3
lend in (24)
were taken over (20)
is concerned with (5–6)
rediscounted by (64)
means the same as
rediscounted with (81)
is used for (51)

call for (94)

B   Notice the difference between *in* and *on*:

lend in deal in pay in (p. 109 **A**)	cash, kind, hundis, pounds, dollars, kind or form of money
lend on pay on	a date or terms of business

C   Use the verbs in the three lists to complete the following passage. Use each verb once only. The verbs are listed in random order. Be careful to put the verbs in the right form:

List 1
The short-term money market, part of which is sometimes (1)_____
_____ 'the overnight market', should be (2)_____ _____ the
medium- and long-term markets in that money (3)_____ _____
_____ a day-to-day basis and interest rates (4)_____ _____
_____ the availability of liquid resources and the immediate needs of
the banks which (5)_____ each other _____ money to balance their
books at the end of the day.

List 2
The medium-term market, on the other hand, (6)_____ mainly
_____ Bills of Exchange and is not (7)_____ so much _____ the

hands of the banks. One can (8)_____   _____ two major types of
Bill: Treasury Bills and commercial or bank Bills. The former
(9)_____   _____ Bills issued by the government to obtain money
for its current account expenditure. The system in London differs from
that of other countries because the banks do not (10)_____ directly
_____ the government.

List 3

   Early in the nineteenth century that function (11)_____   _____
_____ from the Bill Brokers by the discount houses which act as
intermediaries between the Treasury and the banks which want to
(12)_____   _____ a safe market for short periods. The discount
houses are exclusively (13)_____   _____ the short-term money
supply. The Treasury (14)_____ them _____ providing instant liquid
funds. On the other hand, if the market is short of liquid money, the
banks can easily (15)_____ the Bills _____ the central bank.

D   Payable on sight Study the way the following phrases are used in
the passage:

inherent in (38 and 40)
payable *on* sight/presentation/(demand) (50)
payable *at* 90 days/30 days/short notice (53)
similar to (59)   dependent on (72)
questionable whether (76)   apart from (82)

E   Use the phrases in D above to complete the following:

In contrast with negotiable instruments, the obligation of the drawee to
pay is not (1)_____   _____ cheques. A cheque is (2)_____
_____ an I.O.U. and its value is entirely (3)_____   _____ the
value of the guarantee of the bank which may or may not be given. But
it is (4)_____   _____ a Bill of Exchange would be paid unless it was
accepted by a well-known bank. The difference is that, (5)_____
_____ unaccepted Bills, the payee can demand payment from any
signatory to the Bill and this includes the drawee. Another difference
between cheques and Bills of Exchange is that the latter can be made
(6)_____   _____ demand or (7)_____   _____ a varying number
of days after sight.

F   With the support of . . . (21). Notice how the following nouns are
used in the passage:

access to (36)	connection between (78)
in the sense of (39)	(the connection *between* x and y)
in contrast with (54)	connection with
days' grace (54)	(x's connection *with* y)
contact between (67)	

G   Use the phrases in F above to complete the following sentences:

1 It is important for all employees to have _____   _____ the
   manager.
2 The _____   _____ the banks and the government is supervised
   by the central bank.
3 The drawee of a Bill usually has _____   _____   _____ to pay.
4 _____   _____   _____ a Bill, a cheque is not normally
   negotiable.

Self-assessment

A   Answer the questions below without looking at the previous pages:

marks

1 In answering an essay question, where is it best to put your short answer?
  a at the beginning   **b** in the middle   **c** towards the end   (1)

2 Question analysis is concerned with mapping out the _____ of the question as well as the communicative function of the answer.   **a** topics   **b** purpose   **c** paragraphs   (1)

3 Question analysis is helpful because it helps you to _____ your answer.   **a** arrange   **b** organise   **c** improve   (1)

4 If a paragraph contains a number of points leading to a generalisation, its organisation is _____
  a deductive   **b** inductive   **c** collective   (1)

5 If a paragraph contains a generalisation followed by several supporting pieces of evidence, its organisation is _____
  a deductive   **b** inductive   **c** collective   (1)

6 The ancient credit instruments of India are similar to _____
  a cheques   **b** securities   **c** promissory notes   (1)

7 Which of the money markets is the indigenous banking system *not* concerned with?   **a** long term   **b** medium term   **c** short term   (1)

8 Rewrite one of the following sentences without the word *which*:
  a A study of the traditional rural credit systems which have been used in India may help us to solve problems of agricultural development.
  b A study of the traditional rural credit systems which have existed in India for centuries may help us to solve the problems of agricultural development.   (3)

9 Write out the following, putting the verb (in brackets) in the correct form:
  Loans from private bankers (can obtain) by personal contact and with less formality than from the public banks.   (2)

10 Rewrite the following sentence using *although*:
  Despite the spread of modern banks to most parts of the country, the traditional sector continues to play a major role in rural credit.   (4)

11 Rewrite the following sentence using *despite*:
  Although the financial system is advanced, the problem of rural development is acute.   (4)

12 Supply one word for each space:
  The traditional bankers are _____ on the joint-stock banks to _____ their hundis if they are short of _____ . So there is a connection _____ the national banking system. Apart from this, however, the public sector banks do not normally deal _____ hundis.   (5)

Total (25)

B   Check your answers in the Answer Key.

Unit 12 Banking and development: Agricultural credit

Preview

In this unit we will

1 collect topics from a selection of exam questions

2 organise the topics into a conceptual framework

3 make notes relating to questions

4 identify redundant parts of a text

5 study technical banking terms used in a fresh context

6 look at good and bad ways of starting essays

7 practise using the right participle or preposition after some verbs

8 practise shortening sentences and writing briefly

Preparing to read and write

Collecting topics

Collecting topics on Agricultural Credit (Surveying the subject and coverage)

Pick out the main topic areas of the following questions:

1 Describe the role of bank credit in the distribution of income and wealth.
(*Economics*, Banking Diploma, I, Institute of Bankers, Pakistan, May 1982.)

2 Distinguish between modernisation and mechanisation of agriculture and describe briefly the part played by credit in both processes, in achieving self-sufficiency in food grains.
(*Agricultural Credit*, Banking Diploma, I, Institute of Bankers, Pakistan, May 1982)

3 It is said that fragmentation of land holdings is one of the biggest constraints in the development of agriculture in the country. How far can it be checked by regulatory measures, such as land reform, or by the process of agricultural development itself?
(*Agricultural Credit*, Banking Diploma, I, Institute of Bankers, Pakistan, May 1982)

4 a What are the major objectives of economic planning in your country?
  b Do you think your country has been successful in economic planning?
(Adapted from *Malaysian Economic & Financial Environment*, Banking Diploma, I, Malaysian Institute of Bankers, September 1981.)

5 a What are the costs and benefits of promoting industrialisation in your country?

b What are the problems your country is likely to face in speeding up industrialisation?

(Adapted from *Malaysian Economic & Financial Environment*, Banking Diploma, I, Malaysian Institute of Bankers, September 1981)

6 What do you understand by 'project evaluation' in banking? Explain what you mean, using an example of a project in your own country.

7 Under what circumstances should:

a repayment installments be postponed?

b accumulated repayment installments be rescheduled?

c accumulated interest be partly written off?

d the entire overdue repayments be written off as irrecoverable?

(*Agricultural Credit*, Banking Diploma, I, Institute of Bankers, Pakistan, December 1981)

8 Should agricultural insurance for crops as well as for livestock be introduced in the country? If so, suggest a mechanism for it.

(*Agricultural Credit*, Banking Diploma, I, Institute of Bankers, Pakistan, May 1982)

9 Discuss the merits of accepting immovable properties as security for agricultural loans.

(*Agricultural Credit*, Banking Diploma, I, Institute of Bankers, Pakistan, May 1982)

10 'In many countries laws forbid the marriage of commercial and investment banking, although it is sometimes doubtful that the banks would make longer term commitments even if they could, in view of the large and profitable demands for other kinds of business.'

Discuss the position in your country.

(*Industrial Credit & Investment*, Banking Diploma, I, Institute of Bankers, Pakistan, May 1982)

Organising topics

Organising topics into a conceptual framework (Surveying the organisation of the subject)

A   From the following list of topics pick out one which covers all the above questions and write it in box 1 on page 129:

agricultural credit	credit losses
credit security	project evaluation
commercial banking	industrial development banking
investment banking	mechanisation of agriculture
savings banks	modernisation of agriculture
land reform	social responsibility
economic development	development banking

B   Now complete the concept table with other items from the list of topics above.

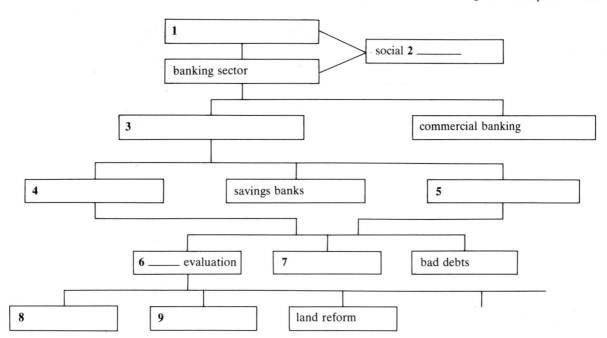

Reading and making notes

A   Your reading purpose is to extract information from a text and make notes on it in order to answer a question. First, study the following questions on agricultural credit:

1 What are the problems of agricultural credit in a developing country? What solutions can be put forward to solve them?

2 Describe the role of the middleman in the marketing of at least two agricultural commodities. Can he be replaced by credit banks or other institutions?
(*Agricultural Credit*, Banking Diploma, Institute of Bankers, Pakistan, Winter 1981)

3 What are the functions of a development bank? Illustrate your answer with one example from your region.
(Adapted from *Economics*, West African Secondary Certificate and GCE, June, 1981)

4 Why do commercial banks in your country play a relatively small role in financing economic development?

B Make a list of topic headings under which you would make notes to answer the above questions.

C Make notes on the two reading passages which follow, organising them under the topic headings you have listed. If you are working in a class, you could share out the work among groups or pairs – each group making notes on one question and its component topics. Compare notes afterwards.

Reading passage A *Financing peasant agriculture*

A In this passage there is a lot of redundancy, i.e. repetition of what has already been said. The information in the passage is not concentrated and you should be able to read it more quickly than earlier passages.

B Answer the questions on the left.

1 *autonomy* (7) = entertainment? independence? free transport?

2 What words in this paragraph show that the writer is putting forward suggestions?

3 What is the main point of paragraph 3?

4 *crown land* (17) = government land? good quality land? land for money?

5 *title* (19) = honour? name? legal ownership?

6 *equitable* (23) = equal? fair? big?

7 Why will a *tripartite agreement* (26) be necessary? (Look ahead in the text.)

8 What does this sentence (31–2) explain?

9 Which part of the tripartite agreement does *capitalist* (34) refer to?

The development of the rural sector is necessary not only to reduce the pressure of population migrations to the cities but also to achieve the diffusion of wealth and incomes in the country as a whole . . .

5 Agricultural credit has always been risky . . . It is equally true that those who borrow from government institutions that do not enjoy any real autonomy in practice tend to view credit as grants or gifts rather than as loans that must be repaid in accordance with the terms agreed

10 upon. What is therefore required, among other things, are elaborate schemes of supervised credit through autonomous financing institutions.

In those developing countries that are committed to a mixed economy, one solution would be to establish in

15 strategic centers, insofar as it is practicable, a multipurpose joint-stock company, preferably broadly based, to which extensive agricultural crown land could be given on 30 years' lease. Additionally, peasants could be given five acres or more with absolute title to their land with the

20 provision that, if the land is neglected, the joint-stock company would take possession of the land, make it productive, and later–three years, perhaps–hand over possession to the peasant in return for payment of an equitable sum, perhaps under an installment payment basis, to meet the

25 costs incurred in maintaining or developing the land. It will be necessary to arrange for a tripartite agreement among the government, the joint-stock company, and the small landholder, under which modern methods of agriculture would be introduced where necessary by the company so as

30 to demonstrate the advantages of these methods to the peasants. The peasants' interests need to be safeguarded, as do those of the joint-stock company.

A scheme of this type would go a long way in ensuring capitalist–peasant participation in modernizing agriculture

35 and farming. At the same time, it would give agriculture and farming a respectable image and thus discourage

10 Why do people migrate to the cities?

11 Find the sentence in paragraph 3 which means the same as the words in italics.

appropriate (41) = correct, right for the purpose

12 Find an expression in paragraph 3 equivalent to *permanent ownership* (44).

13 How does the writer show he is moving to a different aspect of the same idea? (47)

14 What organisation might supply the *expertise* (50)?

15 *pool* (51) = water? put together? plough?

16 *viable* (52) = sensible? workable? profitable?

17 Who should encourage them?

18 Why should peasants want to move from one area to another?

reverted (67) = gone back to

19 *incentives* (69) = rewards? freedom? increases?
expropriate (70) = taken away from (*ex* = out of, away from + *appropriate* = take possession of)

20 *on the grounds that* (71) = for the reasons that? on the land that?

migrations into urban areas. The foregoing would apply to extensive land that is leased to joint-stock companies and small lots sold outright to peasants who have title to them,
40 *with the condition that the possession of the land will temporarily pass to appropriate joint-stock companies, if the land remains either undeveloped or underdeveloped.* The main purpose of this arrangement is to enable the peasant to feel a sense of almost permanent ownership of his land,
45 and thus to motivate him to manage his property with greater care than before.*

Somewhat similar schemes could be introduced in areas where agricultural land in small lots is held by peasant cultivators under freehold title. These small holders, who are
50 too small to obtain adequate credit and expertise, should be encouraged to pool their lands voluntarily in order to develop economically viable units under the supervision of a company-type organization similar to the one already described . . .
55 During the off-season periods of the year, peasants will obviously be unemployed or underemployed and may become heavily indebted. It is during these periods that the company organizations, in cooperation with other capitalist organizations engaged in industry in that region, should
60 be encouraged to operate certain agro-based industries and other suitable activities more intensely in that region by hiring unemployed and underemployed peasants as temporary workers. An imaginative transportation system to make it easy for peasants to move from one area to
65 another . . .

* In many developing countries, government lands allocated to peasants have reverted to government, because the peasants concerned neglected their lands. In some countries, large areas of government land taken on lease by capitalist groups under very attractive tax incentives,
70 and developed successfully, have been expropriated by socialist governments on the grounds that the capitalist groups concerned had exploited the peasant community living around them.

Reading passage B   *Agricultural finance*

A   Read the passage.

B   Answer the questions on the left.

Expressions of particular use to bankers are in **bold** type.

1 What antonym binds the first half of this sentence to the second?

2 What does *imbalance* (3) refer to?

3 *marshal* (4) = collect? deliver? transport?

4 What's the opposite of *rural* (5)?

5 How many *alternatives* (5) are mentioned? What are they?

6 Why has *tough out* (10) been put in inverted commas?

7 Which word could be replaced by *determination*?

8 Is the argument in this paragraph deductive or inductive?

9 Summarise the argument in note form.

10 Think of an equivalent for '*hard*' (18).

11 What is meant by '*soft*' lending (18–19)?

12 *fritter away* (19) = use up? cook up? waste in small amounts?

13 **Why is** *Treasury* (23) spelt with a capital T?

14 Why has this section been indented?

15 *arrears* (29) of what?

16 *winding up* (31) = bringing to an end? renewing its strength? speeding up?

sic (32) = thus (The form of the verb, though incorrect, has been reproduced as written.)

17 *onslaught* (35) = solution? entertainment? attack?

18 Who bears the loss in the end? Who are the 'end losers'?

The **volume of savings flowing** to financial institutions from rural areas is small while the **credit needs** of peasant producers are great. This imbalance has rendered impractical the desires of many governments to marshal rural savings
5 and lend them to rural producers. The alternatives of **injecting** into the rural area **funds** raised from urban dwellers, or from **foreign loans**, or by taxation have generally failed for the want of sufficient government recognition of the difficulties involved in supplying agricultural credit,
10 and the consequent lack of resolution to 'tough out' the inevitably long period of initial unprofitability associated with credit provided for the modernization of traditional agriculture. The fundamental problem is that any financial institution or system which sets out to **meet the needs** of
15 small-scale rural producers, and which aims to be self-sufficient, requires (1) **access to savings** from outside the agricultural sector as **a major source of funds**, and (2) a 'hard' banking attitude towards rural loans, for 'soft' lending will only fritter away loanable funds without impressing
20 upon the peasants the true value of capital or improving the productivity of their farming.

The proper approach to small-scale agricultural credit is well illustrated in the following statement by a Treasury official:
25   We are lending here to a large mass of people who are essentially, in a banking sense, not **credit-worthy**. This is why government provides this credit; and, in the very nature of the scheme financed, I think we have to accept the fact that there are bound to be **arrears**. To adopt a
30   purely legalistic approach to this scheme would merely lead to its **winding up** in one year at **considerable loss** and also to defeat [*sic*] the government's policy of trying to improve the position of the rural cultivators. (quoted in Drake, 1966, p. 81)
35 If a large-scale onslaught on the rural credit problem is desired, government must lead the way, for there are bound to be losses and only government should be expected to **underwrite losses** in the interests of rural betterment. A developing economy cannot afford failures among
40 financial institutions, for such might destroy the confidence

19 Re-write the metaphor *play fairy godmother* (42) in other words.

20 *integral* (45) = distant? controlling? necessary part of life?

21 What word does the writer use to emphasise what he is saying?

22 What are the implications of this proposal for the traditional financial sector?

23 Why are inverted commas used for these two expressions (58 and 59–60)?

24 These organisations would have to _____ the bills.

occasioned (66) = caused

25 What is new about this proposed use of bill finance?

26 What words show that the foregoing proposals are only suggestions?

27 Write a sentence to paraphrase *the line of investigation seems promising* 75–6).

28 Who would be the providers of *informal credit* (78–9)?

29 What is the antonym for *borrow* (81) in this sentence?

30 Find a synonym for *lack of will* (81).

31 Why would a government be interested in a *local outlet for the savings of other sectors* (84–5)?

32 What paper (85)?

33 *Range of maturities* (87) of what?

of many people in the money and credit system. However, not even government should play fairy godmother. **Strict supervision** of rural borrowers is needed wherever the credit comes from and however it is distributed.

45   In the rural economy there is an integral relationship between the provision of credit and the processing and the marketing of produce. It is this relationship that is often exploited by middlemen. This same relationship suggests a way in which the government could more effectively assist
50   the small rural producers. A government marketing authority could supply seasonal credit to agriculturalists, or to local buyers of produce, against the future (compulsory) delivery of produce. (The marketing authority would thus be either competing against informal village money-
55   lenders or providing them with the opportunity to expand the scale of their activities.) The funds to **finance** the marketing authority could be obtained by the **issue, under guarantee**, of '**rural produce bills**' (and, where **long-term credit** for capital formation is needed, '**rural development**
60   **bonds**'). With a guarantee that was virtually that of government, banks and other finance houses, including **urban co-operative credit societies**, might then be encouraged to **hold** such bills. The bills would be especially attractive if they were **rediscountable** at the central bank. Of course,
65   the government, through the marketing authority, would have to assume responsibility for losses, occasioned by non-delivery of produce. But under this arrangement government would only have to cover losses, not **outlay its own capital** to finance the scheme; and, in the long run, if
70   farm productivity increases and peasants come to place the **meeting of commercial obligations** high on their scale of duties, it may not be too much to expect the loss rate to diminish greatly. Any such scheme would require detailed and careful examination and evaluation to determine its
75   **feasibility** in any actual situation. But the line of investigation seems promising, especially as there would be the associated advantages of providing additional local **financial assets** and perhaps linking informal to institutional credit.

80   In contrast to some other sectors, there is usually no reluctance to borrow or lack of the will to invest in the rural economy. The **issue** of **rural credit bills** or **bonds** would be a means of taking advantage of this willingness to borrow, at the same time providing a **local outlet** for the savings of
85   other sectors. Moreover, since **rural produce paper** would be expected to **yield a higher rate of interest** than **Treasury bills**, and since a **range of maturities** could be designed to

34 *augmented* (89–90) = increased? decreased? controlled?

35 Which words does the writer use to show that he wants to answer an expected objection to his argument? (see also line 64)

ear-mark (95–6) = a method of labelling cattle used by farmers at livestock markets

36 *intangible* (97) = untouchable? insubstantial? not concrete?

37 Whose revenue and expenditure (99–100)?

38 What word shows that another contrasting point of view is about to be mentioned?

39 *simultaneously* (104–5) = properly? at the same time? strongly?

40 What are the implications of the last sentence?

suit different products and methods of production, the variety as well as the supply of local **paper** would be aug-
90   mented. However, the quality of the paper would have to be ensured, because bad bills or bonds would wreck the system; it must be repeated that it would be necessary that the paper be issued or guaranteed by government. Of course, the proposal might be regarded simply as the ex-
95   tension of **government domestic debt** with a portion ear-marked for a specific purpose. But this view overlooks the intangible advantages and political goodwill that should follow from the creation of a recognizably separate authority, with its finances divorced from general revenue and
100   expenditure and with the challenging responsibility to achieve something worthwhile in the rural economy.

Nevertheless, rural underdevelopment is not merely a problem of insufficient finance. There would be no point in increasing the supply of rural credit without simultane-
105   ously tackling the related problems of low productivity and commercial and technical backwardness and, in many cases, the pressure of fast-growing populations on limited land. Innovations and reforms in the financial field are not enough.

Discussion

Ask and answer

A   Ask and answer questions about the following:

1 mixed economy	**7** credit-worthy
2 joint-stock company	**8** underwrite
3 title	**9** rural produce Bills
4 to be in arrears	**10** bonds
5 wind up	**11** rural produce paper
6 range of maturities	**12** domestic debt

examples
definition questions:
What is a mixed economy?
What is the difference between a mixed economy and a state economy?
asking for opinions:
What are the disadvantages of a mixed economy?

B   Ask and answer questions about the main issues in agricultural policy and the problems of agricultural credit **a** in the developing countries in general, and **b** in specific countries. Whenever possible, refer to situations which you know about in your own country. The following notes will help you:

1 national food production policy
2 food imports/food exports

What . . . . . . in (country)?
What are the main . . . in . . .?

3 private sector banks or government
4 small size of peasant holdings
5 government policy on . . .
6 the role of the middleman
7 land reform policy
8 modernisation
9 mechanisation
10 migration to the cities
11 decline of interest in farming
12 the state of agricultural production

Do/Does . . . in . . . participate?
Is . . . a problem in . . .?
What . . . in . . .?
What is . . . in . . .?
Is there . . . in . . .?
How successful is . . .?
. . . advantages/disadvantages . . .?
Is . . . in . . . increasing/decreasing?
Is there a . . . . . . in . . .?
What . . . in . . . . . .?

C   Further discussion Continue your discussion on the subject: The role of international trade in food production in Europe and the USA.

Analysis

Preparing to write

A   Relating to the question Read question 1 on page 127 again. Then read the opening sentences for essays in answer to it (**1–6** below) and think about the criticisms which follow them:

1 If a farmer wanted to buy a tractor, he could borrow the money from the bank.
(This answer has no specific bearing on the question. The farmer might already be rich, so borrowing from the bank would have no effect on the distribution of wealth.)

2 If someone wanted to borrow money from his bank, this would help to distribute wealth into his account.
(This is a trivial example because the question is about distribution of wealth in general, not about the position of an individual's personal wealth.)

3 Bank credit helps to distribute wealth by ensuring that people's salaries and wages are credited to their accounts and debited from the accounts of their employers.
(This sentence is confused in two ways. The distribution of wages into people's bank accounts is not the same as the distribution of wealth and is a separate matter from bank credit.)

4 The most important factor in ensuring good consumer demand is the availability of credit. This may be obtained from a hire purchase company or from your own bank.
(This appears to be answering a question about consumer purchasing power, rather than about the distribution of wealth.)

5 All banks have a duty to distribute wealth to the poor. This should be accomplished by having joint ventures and giving easy terms to the developing countries.
(This says what, in the writer's opinion, the banks ought to do and not what actually happens. The writer of this sentence is using the wrong function, although the topic is relevant.)

6 Bank credit plays a very important role in the distribution of wealth.
(This is a waste of time and effort because it doesn't do what the queston asks. It simply restates the question in the form of a value judgement.)

The criticisms can be summed up as follows:

1 starting with a vague example
2 starting with a trivial example
3 confusing ideas with a separate issue
4 exchanging the question; answering a completely different imaginary question
5 altering the question; the writer is bending the question to enable him to sound off his/her views
6 unnecessary repetition of the question

B Now discuss the following opening sentences to essays. What is wrong with them? (They are in answer to the numbered questions on pp. 127–8.)

Question 2
There is no doubt that many governments, in their efforts to modernise their industries, have neglected the agricultural sector.

Question 3
Despite the division of land into many small units, it is possible to achieve a high degree of agricultural development.

Question 4
Quite recently the government of _____ wasted a lot of money building a four lane motorway from _____ to _____ when a two lane one would have served the purpose.

Question 5
_____ (name of country) will gain immensely from industrialisation but there are several factors hindering progress.

Question 6
Quite recently the government has encouraged the banks to open new branches all over the country following a recent positive evaluation of the project.

Check your criticisms against those in the Answer Key.

C Reducing sentence length The long sentences you frequently read in textbooks and articles are usually written by people who have a mastery of English. Do not attempt to imitate them because, unless your English is perfect, you will make grammatical mistakes which make it difficult for your reader to understand what you are saying. It is advisable to keep sentences as short as possible. Good style can be achieved with short sentences and there are many great modern writers who have proved this.

In Unit 10 you had practice in dividing sentences up into sense units. This should help you to break down your own sentences into smaller units. Continuity should be maintained by using connecting reference words like those studied in Units 2 and 7.

D Look at the following examples of how sentences from reading passage A can be broken down into shorter units and made more straightforward.

Financing peasant agriculture (Passage A)
Rewritten form of
1 lines 5–10
It is equally true that many borrowers do not enjoy any real
autonomy. *They* tend to view credits as grants rather than as loans
that must be repaid according to agreed terms.

2 lines 13–18
One solution in mixed economies would be to set up multi-purpose,
broadly based joint-stock companies in strategic centres. *These* could
be given extensive areas of government land on 30 years' leases.

3 lines 18–25
Additionally peasants could be given 5-acre parcels of freehold land.
But a condition would be that *the company* would take it over if *they*
neglected *it*. *The company* would then make *it* productive and after
three years sell *it* back to the peasants on an installment basis. *The
money* would go towards the cost of development.

NOTE
a Avoid unnecessary repetition.
b Make full use of words which connect the sentence you are writing to
your previous sentences. These words (which are italicised in the
above examples) have been referred to frequently in previous units.

E   Practice Rewrite the following sentences from Passage A in shorter
sentences. Keep to the same meaning as much as possible:

1 lines 25–31
2 lines 37–42
3 lines 68–72

**Using the correct
particle**

Necessary to reduce . . . Choose the correct particle or preposition in
the following sentences. (When no preposition or particle is required,
the answer should be 0):

Passage A
  1 This is necessary to/for/0 reduce the pressure of population
     migrations.
  2 They tend to view loans for/in/as gifts.
  3 Some countries are committed for/with/to a mixed economy.
  4 The company would take possession over/by/of the land.
  5 They would hand it up/over/out in return of/for/0 payment.
  6 The scheme would go a long way to/in/for ensuring participation.
  7 It would apply to/for/over large areas of land.
  8 Similar schemes could be introduced with/between/in areas of small
     holdings.
  9 Land could be allocated for/to/among peasants.
 10 The company is engaged in/to/by a joint venture.
 11 The peasants should be able to take on/over/up seasonal work.

Passage B
 12 Funds should be injected in/at/into agricultural production.
 13 Such projects often fail for/in/by want of support by the peasants.
 14 One problem associated to/in/with this type of credit is delayed
     repayments.

15 It would be necessary to impress 0/over/upon the peasants the need to modernise their farming methods.
16 We can suggest to/as/0 a way to solve the problem.
17 Credit banks would compete against/with/over the village money-lender.
18 They should provide to/0/with the farmers 0/to/with incentives to increase their productivity.
19 One would have to take advantage to/of/by this willingness on the part of the farmers to borrow.
20 The issue of rural credit Bills would be a means to take/to taking/of taking advantage of this willingness to borrow.

Extension

Develop your word-power

A Opposites

In Passage A on pages 130–1, find the converse or opposite expressions for the following expressions. The paragraph given is the one where the answer will be found.

examples	*paragraph*	*answer in the text*
cities concentration	1	rural sector diffusion
1 dependence	1	_____
2 simple		_____
3 problem	2	_____
4 looked after		_____
5 outmoded		_____
6 put at risk		_____
7 competition	3	_____
8 prevent		_____
9 temporary		_____
10 insufficient	4	_____
11 divide up		_____
12 co-operatives	footnote	_____

B Equivalents – using your own expressions

Good style does not mean you should use long, flowery expressions. When you write, use ordinary day-to-day words. These simple equivalents are more powerful than elaborate phrases and will enable you to express your ideas better. In Passage B, on pages 132–4, find expressions which could be replaced by the following. Line numbers are given to help you:

examples	*lines*	*answers in the text*
banks	1–10	financial institutions
farmers	1–10	peasant producers
1 made (one word)	1–10	. . .
2 because of a failure to understand the problems	5–15	. . .
3 lending money to smallholders	5–15	. . .
4 the resulting unwillingness	5–15	. . .

5 lending to smallholders   10–20   . . .
6 needs to raise capital elsewhere   10–20   . . .
7 help farmers   30–40   . . .
8 help farmers   45–55   . . .

C   Think up simple equivalent expressions of your own for the following ones from the text. Line references are given.

Passage A
1 achieve the diffusion (one word) (3)

Passage B
2 rural producers (5)
3 assume responsibility for (66)
4 occasioned by (66)
5 meeting of commercial obligations (71)
6 place . . . high on their scale of duties (70)
7 the associated advantages (77)
8 there is usually no reluctance (80)

Answering the question

A   **How to write the first paragraph** Always answer the question *in the first paragraph* of your essay. Start by giving a brief answer in general terms. The subsequent paragraphs should consist of the supporting evidence or arguments. Look at the following examples of ways in which you might start to answer the questions on pages 127–8:

Question 1
Bank credit plays a major role in the distribution of income and wealth. This applies to consumers as well as to small businesses. It also has a 'filter down' effect on the poor.

Bank credit plays a minor role in the distribution of income. It only facilitates further spending by the well-off and barely affects the poor.

Bank credit has no effect at all on the distribution of wealth although many like to think that it improves the position of the poor.

Question 2
NOTE   This is a complicated question but it is essential to map out your answer as simply as possible in the first paragraphs:

Modernisation and mechanisation of agriculture overlap to a certain extent but they should not be confused. A farm may be modernised without being mechanised in that the farmer may use scientific methods of soil conservation, cultivation and animal husbandry without the aid of machines. Conversely, another farmer might be fully mechanised but continue to practise medieval ideas of agriculture.

     The question of whether _____ (name of country) can be self-sufficient in grains depends on the productivity and efficiency of farmers. Long-term credit is indispensable in bringing this about.

Question 3
Experience has shown that there is little governments can do to prevent the fragmentation of land holdings. However, agriculture could be better developed if small farmers were given incentives to work together . . .

Question 4

The major objectives of economic planning in _____ (name of country) are an increase of per capita income, improvement and extension of the infrastructure and the elimination of absolute poverty. So far the government has not been very successful in achieving these aims, although there has been a 5% increase in the GNP over the past three years.

Question 5

The costs of promoting industrialisation in _____ need not be great. It depends on the sort of industrialisation that is decided upon. Certain forms of industry may be relatively cheap to finance, especially if they are self-financed as much as possible. The main problem is that of repaying the country's debts against a background of stagnant productivity and increasing population. Industrialisation, if it means the purchase of capital goods, would result in an increase of these debts.

The immediate benefits of course, are mainly social. In the long term, there would be economic improvements. But the new industries would have to be appropriate to the needs of the country.

B   Practice Write opening paragraphs answering the questions on page 129 as briefly as possible. Use the information in passages A and B, 'Financing peasant agriculture' and 'Agricultural finance'.

Self-assessment

Answer the questions below without looking back at the previous pages:

marks

1 Passage A should be easier to understand than Passage B because it
   a is shorter   **b** repeats similar ideas   **c** has fewer technical expressions   (2)

2 True or false?
   a Passage A deals with agricultural credit mainly from the point of view of the organisation of rural production.
   b Passage A deals with agricultural credit mainly from the point of view of the organisation of finance.
   c Passage B is mainly about how to lend to farmers on a national scale.   (3)

3 Supply one word for each space. (More than one answer is possible in some cases):
   Investment in agriculture is totally (a)_____ for the needs of development. (b)_____ situation makes government attempts to (c)_____ agriculture using rural savings impractical. (d)_____ schemes for using urban savings (e)_____ taxation have usually failed because (f)_____ don't understand the problems involved. (g)_____ don't realise that rural investment (h)_____ long term and no returns (i)_____ capital will be realised for (j)_____ years. Furthermore, to satisfy the (k)_____ for credit, capital from outside (l)_____

is needed. Also one would (m)_____ to train farmers to adopt a (n)_____ business-like attitude to loans.

(o)_____ best way to approach the (p)_____ is to recognise that one (q)_____lending to people who are (r)_____ uncreditworthy. There will be some (s)_____ . But it would defeat the (t)_____ of the government to apply (u)_____ credit rules and some flexibility (v)_____ be necessary. Otherwise the whole (w)_____ of agricultural credit would collapse (x)_____ major losses.   (24)

4 Choose the best alternative:
   a There are many difficulties with/of/in supplying rural credit.
   b One needs to have access to/by/into large supplies of capital.
   c Supervision of/to/on the farmers' loans is advisable.   (3)

5 Find a financial expression equivalent to the following:
   a guarantee
   b can be sold back minus the interest
   c units of investment   (3)

Total   (35)

B   Check your answers in the Answer Key. Make sure you understand your mistakes, if any.

Answer key

Unit 1 Commodity money

The passage

D 1 purpose, use
2 medium of exchange, store of value, standard of deferred payment, measure of value
3 restricted
4 the decorative function
5 different
6 carry
7 joined together
8 comes
9 purpose

Discussion

B 1 The following should be considered: Can we separate social factors from economic factors? Could money objects influence people in a way that is separate from their economic value? What about bribes, national symbols on coins, display of money objects to show wealth, 'flashing' money, display of official power through notes and coins?

2 Coins and notes are usually restricted to the countries in which they are officially used; other money objects tend to be similarly restricted to the area where they are acceptable; but gold coins are widely accepted. On the other hand, large denomination notes can be exchanged or even used directly in other countries.

3 Cash in hand gives more credibility than money in the bank; most people think of money as solid objects; cash also has the advantage that its owner cannot be traced (unlike cheques and bank accounts) so it gives its owner anonymity. Other money objects have value in themselves (decorative shells, cigarettes, bronze figures, gold and silver coins etc.). On a desert island it would be more useful to have cows than cash.

4 Yes. No money objects have the qualities of being movable across the world in any quantity at vast speeds (i.e. bank electronic transfers), payable by writing cheques, conveniently calculable in terms of interest and convertibility into other currencies, occupying no space and capable of being created simply by a bank granting a loan.

Analysis

Using 'the'

B 1 Because it shows that something in particular is being referred to: *the Royal Mint* is like the names of institutions, e.g. the Institute of Bankers, the Khyber Rifles, the Council of Ministers; *the highest* follows the rule which says *the* is required before superlatives.
2 *the* is not used because things in general are meant.

C Answers **1**, **4** and **5** are correct.

D Banks in Britain are well distributed in high streets of every town. Even small towns and some large villages have banks. But names of banks do not vary a great deal. Hundreds of banks that existed long ago have been amalgamated into four huge companies.

E 1 The currency . . . the afghani . . . The people . . . the Afghans . . . the invasion . . . the money-changer . . . the next money-changer . . .

2 The social uses . . . The rich . . . the size . . . the display (optional *the*) . . . The display (optional *the*) . . . the small size . . . the bank accounts . . .

F Most uses of *the* are to indicate that a particular instance of the thing is referred to. But *in the past* (l. 9) is a set expression.

Singular or plural?

C	1 are	5 ways	9 has
	2 examples	6 these	10 they
	3 They	7 forms	11 do
	4 are	8 do	12 units

Punctuation

B Commas after
1 object,   3 considered,
2 money,   4 value,

Use of the past tense

C came, were, was, totalled, changed, withdrew, remained, amounted to, stands, is

Extension

Vocabulary

B 1 specialised   4 country of origin
2 restricted   5 combined
3 limited

Converting notes into text

B **3** Conus shells were kept on a string in the form of a necklace. This was a useful way of carrying small change around in New Guinea.

4 Flying fox jaws were worn as a sign of peace as well as a purse. They were used for peace-making ceremonies in Fiji.

5 Chung ch'ien, or 'bell cash', had magical value and were used as marriage gifts in China during the Han period. They were an example of special purpose money.

6 In Roman Britain cattle were used as blood-money. In Roman law, compensation for breaking a bone of a free man was set at 300 donkeys and for a slave 150 donkeys. The compensation for hitting a free man was 25 donkeys.

7 Iron bar currency was widely used for trade in Nigeria. The bars could also be turned into hoes.

8 In Mycenae, in ancient Greece, gold rings were used as money. Different values could be made by fixing different numbers of rings together.

9 Brass ornaments served the purpose of decoration as well as a medium of exchange in parts of Indonesia.

10 In Japan, various measures of value could be produced with varying amounts of rice.

11 Bronze axe-heads were considered valuable not only as tools but as a medium of exchange in Bronze-Age Germany. Though useful, they were heavy to carry about.

Self-assessment

A **1** Remember SCOPE: ask yourself questions about its subject, coverage, organisation, purpose and examples.
2 Consult **a** your own knowledge of the subject, **b** a fellow student or **c** a textbook or dictionary.
3 The use of money is also influenced by social and religious factors.
4 The notes which we now carry are worth no more than the paper they are printed on. The sentence on the note saying 'I promise to pay the bearer the sum of one pound' only means you can exchange it for another pound note.
5 Until quite recently, even though paper money was more convenient, coins remained more popular.
6 **a** restricted **b** limited
7 Iron bar currency was used in Nigeria for trade. The bars could also be turned into hoes. In 1934, 1 bar was equivalent to 1 penny (25p).

Unit 2 Coin currency

Preparing to read

Surveying the subject

B **3** (other uses of coins): for phone calls, slot machines, tossing up at a football match, opening a bottle, the game of shove ha'penny, as a screwdriver
4 copper, cupro-nickel, aluminium, lead, tin, silver, gold
5 kings, queens, national figures, leaders
6 national symbols, political symbols (crowns, hammer & sickle, wheel of life, etc.)

The passage

C **1** other forms of commodity money
2 national money
3 going round among the people
4 world-wide
5 qualities
6 signs
7 amounts

D **1** c **2** b **3** b & c
4 Coins are solid, attractive, hard-wearing and easy to handle; they carry official authority, represent law and order and are available in values useful for shopkeepers.
5 They represent peace, law, order and stability.
6 The head of the ruler, or head of state, is shown on the coin.
7 a

Analysis

Connecting words

C **1** They **3** which **5** this **7** it
2 these **4** them **6** It

Word families

B **1** **a** precious metals **b** gold **c** copper **d** lead
2 **a** empress **b** kings
3 2,300

C **1** cows **2** donkeys **3** livestock **4** pigs

D **1** injury **3** bones **5** killing
2 breaking **4** hitting a man **6** breaking an arm

Connecting words: sets

D **1** rider **3** gallop **5** security
2 saddle-bag **4** bandit **6** crime

E Horsemanship and Crime are the two headings involved.

Connecting words: equivalences
B **1** e **2** c **3** d **4** a **5** b

Using verbs

B 1 . . . these metals were used to mint money.
2 A new cheque book with my name on it was issued . . .
3 A system of payment by bank cards was tried out . . .
4 After the purchase has been completed, a card is inserted into . . .
5 Several machines were fitted into shops . . .
6 Some years ago a similar experiment was tried out in California . . .
7 . . . your bank card is rejected in the shop in front of other people.
8 . . . the system was not accepted by the public.
9 The scheme was withdrawn . . .

Extension

Word study

B Credit cards as a method of payment are widely accepted in the USA. Made from a hard-wearing form of plastic, they fit easily into a wallet . . . The cards are well known all over the world

Self-assessment

A 1 Survey the subject by asking and answering questions about it.
2 To get a rough idea of the contents so as to prepare yourself to understand it better when you read it more carefully.
3 a   4 b   5 a & b   6 b & c
7 **a** The machines in the French shops are/were operated in much the same way as cash points outside banks in Britain.
b After the cash card has been inserted, the personal number is typed from memory on the machine's keyboard.
8 **a** Hard-wearing metals are usually used to mint coins.   **b** Dollars are widely accepted for payment in international trade.
9 Advantages: acceptable in different countries, maintain value, attractive, hard-wearing, high denomination possible with gold. Disadvantages: heavy, risky to carry around, can be debased, inconvenient to move about in large amounts, too valuable for small purchases, dependent on supply of metals

Unit 3 Money in modern economics

Preparing to read

A 1 Add to the list: expensive to manufacture; convertible to other uses; value of the metal can vary from the face value of the coin

2 Properties important to modern money: international acceptability; recognisability; difficult to forge
3 Properties acting as a hindrance to using as modern money: sought after as a commodity; heavy; expensive to insure; difficult to transport

B 1 base metal coins: attractive, durable, sought after as a commodity, heavy
2 banknotes: attractive, generally recognisable as money, available in any units of value, difficult to forge
3 bank accounts: internationally acceptable; available in any amounts

C 1 (gold) intrinsic properties: durable, metallic, useful as a commodity, can be produced in attractive designs . . .; extrinsic properties: expensive, recognisable, internationally acceptable, expensive to insure, transport and forge, rarity value . . .
2 (base metal coins) intrinsic properties: durable, useful as a commodity, heavy, brown or grey; extrinsic properties: available in fixed units of value, inexpensive to manufacture, low value, useful for operating slot machines, expensive to transport
3 (bank notes) intrinsic properties: light, portable, attractive, non-durable, inflammable, made of worthless material; extrinsic properties: cheap to manufacture and transport, convenient, available in any denomination, difficult to forge
4 (bank balances) intrinsic properties: non-physical, notional, quantity not related to physical object; extrinsic properties: cost unaffected by quantity, instantly transferable to any part of the world where there is another bank, not liable to ordinary theft, extremely cheap to create, available in any unit of value

D 1 **a** copper, lead, silver, gold, aluminium, zinc, cupro-nickel   **b** wood-pulp, printing ink   **c** no materials
2 **a** smelting, die casting   **b** paper making, printing   **c** none
3 **a** vaults (strong rooms)   **b** bank vaults and cash tills   **c** none
4 physical money such as notes and coins

The passage

C 1 For instance, the actual value of gold and its general merits as a metal is not related to the economic functions of money.
2 The four functions of money commonly mentioned in textbooks on banking (i.e. as a medium of exchange, store of value, standard of deferred payment, measure of value) .
3 less satisfactory than non-physical forms of money (e.g. bank balances)

4 to bring the raw materials to the mints, to distribute notes and coins to the banking system from the Central Bank and to distribute notes and coins among various branches of a single bank

5 in bank tills and vaults and in private safes and bank nightsafes

6 soak up

7 wealth

8 By using less physical money, the cost of minting coins and printing notes and their distribution and counting would be saved.

9 the result of the development of the banking system by which economies in the use of money were made

10 payment

11 all holders of banknotes

Discussion

A 1 b
2 (the name of your national currency)
3 some commodity moneys
4 c
5 economies in the production of money
6 a
7 banknotes
8 bank deposits
9 They can be created by the banks.

Analysis

Vocabulary practice
1 properties
2 real wants
3 stock
4 converted
5 . . . credited his account with the money

What comes next?
A 1 why most payments do not use legal tender

Find the main verb
1 are
2 suffer
3 absorb
4 resulted from
5 was
6 has been
7 can be distinguished from
8 are
9 are
10 are not
11 would be

Generalisations
A 3 medium

B 1 systems
2 moneys
3 use/take
4 resources
5 wants/needs
6 Banks
7 customers
8 payments
9 cheques
10 accounts
11 payees

C attempts, moneys, deposits, notes

Understanding 'but'

B 2 *but* is used to express contrast.
and is used to express addition.

C 1 Money must have value for buying things but it needn't be valuable in itself.
2 Money must have value . . . and it must be generally recognisable as money.
3 Banknotes are legal tender and they must be accepted in . . .
4 . . . but large sums are usually . . .
5 Coins are useful for operating machines and they can be used . . .
6 . . . but they are inconvenient . . .

Test your reasoning

1 a
2 They are awkward to transfer from one country to another as payment in international trade; they require time to count and are therefore inconvenient for large payments; they are less secure than bank deposits.
3 c
4 They aren't easy to lend (one can't lend gold against interest); they get worn by circulation and have to be replaced; costs of storing cash are greater than those of storing bank balances; they take up physical space; they can lose value during inflation.

Sentence structures

B 1 Another point is that there must be economies in the money system.
2 The only thing that counts is that there should be money in our account.
3 An important aspect of banking is that there are economical forms of money.
4 It is essential that there should be convenient coins for ordinary circulation.
5 It is crucial that there must be complete confidence in the currency.

D 1 The point to bear in mind is that commodity moneys are expensive to produce.
2 Another factor is that the banking system must make economies in the money system.
3 It is vital that deposits should be convertible into legal tender at short notice.
4 It is an advantage that bank deposits are very easily transferable.

F 1 It is economical to minimise cash in circulation by persuading the public to use cheques.
2 It is easier to pay larger amounts by writing cheques.
3 It is safer to avoid carrying money around by using cheques.
4 It is advisable to take good care of your bank card by keeping it in a safe place.
5 It is important to keep an eye on your expenditure by completing your cheque book counterfoils.

Self-assessment

A 1 Yes
 2 They are recognisable as money, cheap to print, difficult to forge, available in any units of value, convenient to use, impersonal.
 3 heavy, durable, attractive, easy to work, non-corrosive
 4 raw materials, labour, printing ink, capital goods, printing presses and coin casting machines, transport, storage (+ guards), insurance
 5 c
 6 banknotes that have to be accepted in settlement of debts
 7 plural
 8 but
 9 **a** The fact is that physical money is expensive to produce.
 b The important point is that economies can be achieved by using bank money.
 c It is a simple matter to increase the money supply by printing more banknotes.

Unit 4 Banking indexes and syllabuses

Practice

Comparing lists of topics

C 1 Chs. 3, 12, 15, 16, 17
 2 Chs. 2, 5, 11, 12, 14, 17
 3 Chs. 1, 6
 4 Ch. 12
 5 no reference in list of contents but check index
 6 Ch. 16
 7 Chs. 13, 14, 15
 8 no reference but check index
 9 Chs. 11, 12
 10 check index
 11 check index   **12** Chs. 1, 6, 8

D   Items 6, 7, 8, 9, 10

E   Items 1, 2, 3, 4, 11

Alphabetical order

A 1 ABEFHIJKLNORTU
 2 blue chip, debenture, equity, gilts, goodwill, rights issue, stock, treasury bills

B 1 rate, receiver, risk, royalty, run

C 1 macro-economics, managed bonds, marked cheque, matrix, maximum load line

D 1 tenant, tendance, tenement, tenor, tenure

E 1 withdrawal, withholding tax, without reserve, with profits
 2 good consideration, good faith, good for, goods, goods and chattels

F   Amsterdam-Rotterdam Bank, Associated Japanese Bank, Banco di Roma, Banco do Brasil, Bangkok Bank, Deutsche Bank, Development Bank of Singapore, New Nigeria Bank, Shanghai Commercial Bank, State Bank of India

Using indexes

A 1 Detailed items are indented from the main column of print.
 2 IMF, Indian unemployment, the Industrial Revolution in France
 3 **b** – because there are more references to the Industrial Revolution than to other topics

B   (costing) information, methods, systems and techniques; (costs) allocated and proportioned, classification of, direct and indirect, fixed and variable, labour, marginal

C 1 Look up under Bills of exchange, Cheques, Methods of payment, History of paper money, Law relating to banking, Protesting a Bill, Letters of Credit
 2 Look up under New developments in banking, Credit cards, Other services provided by banks.
 3 Look up under Bank credit, Interest, Finance of companies, Consumer finance, among others.
 4 Look up under Development and Third World banking, Financial economics in Third World countries, Money-lenders, Traditional sector services.
 5 Look up under New developments in banking, Clearing systems, Methods of payment.

Titles and sub-titles

A 1 o   2 f   3 **m** and **p**
 4 Structure: **h, j** and **l**   Evolution: **b** and **k**

Newspaper indexes

A	1	4	5	4	9	7 & 8	13	29
	2	4	6	2, 3 & 4	10	28	14	25–27
	3	7 & 8	7	29	11	29	15	26
	4	14	8	34	12	4	16	25–27

B 1 Commodities   7 Overseas News
 2 Foreign Exchanges   8 European News
 3 Stock Markets, London   9 Stock Markets, Wall Street
 4 UK News, Labour
 5 Technology   10 Appointments, International
 6 Base Rates

Analysis

'the' again

D 1 Third World countries are now paying back more money to the banks than the banks are lending them, according to the president of the World Bank.
 2 Speaking to the European Management Forum, he said there was a net drain of $21 billion to the rest of the world.

3 The outflow of funds from the Third World, mainly caused by repayments of high interest loans, is much higher than the (optional) recent estimates made by commercial banks.

4 The transfer refers to new lending minus debt service payments on medium- and long-term lending from the private sector.

5 The figures must be set against the ones published earlier this week by the Bank for International Settlements.

Capital letters

1 Mr Clausen warned that it would take years to repair the damage done to Third World prospects by the worst recession in forty years.

2 The bank's affiliate, the International Development Association, had just agreed a $9 billion funding.

3 The International Monetary Fund expects this April's meeting of its policy-making interim committee to go ahead.

4 Although the US Treasury Secretary, Mr Donald Regan, said on Wednesday that he was quite willing to attend the meeting, which has been on the calendar since September, US officials are cool to the idea.

5 They believe the occasion will be used by France and some developing countries to push for a new allocation of special drawing rights, the IMF currency.

Formality

1 The Bank of England has been banker to the government for hundreds of years.

2 The government abandoned the project when they found out about the criminals who had organised it.

3 The manager decided to approve the loan after a talk with the customer who gave him all the details of the project.

4 The exporter should ask his bank to send the documents and whatever else is needed together with the Bill of Exchange to the customer through his bank.

5 Several economic co-operation groups, for instance the EEC, ASEAN and LAFTA, aimed to abolish all import duties on each other's goods.

Sentences from headlines

A (NOTE The sentences in A and B can be written in more than one way. Check your answers with your teacher.)

1 Last night the dollar remained weak but the pound was strong in the European centres.

2 This year the Australian harvest was sharply down compared to last year.

3 A government enquiry has just started into the merger of Barklouds and Bigloans banks.

4 Pressure on banks to cut lending rates has increased this week in New York and London.

5 Production is to end at the Mary Kathleen uranium mine in South Australia following the exhaustion of deposits.

B 1 Several Commonwealth and African loans were proposed in a meeting of finance ministers on Monday.

2 A consortium to be called the Indian Instruments Group, concerned with medical and educational equipment, is to be formed.

3 With adequate support from the City, Lundop can survive, said the new chairman, Sir Hardy Bouncer, at an opening ball last night.

4 In a lightning raid, a Westminster gang cleaned out the strongroom of a branch of the Co-operative Bank, during the early hours of this morning.

Self-assessment

A 1 coverage

2 drachma, draft, draw down, drawer, drawn

3 The major items are printed in line with the main column of the index, while sub-headings are indented.

4 Try to find the item under another heading: think of another expression for the word you want to look up and look it up under this expression; find the section of the book which deals with what you want to know and skim through that section . . .

5 b

6 Soviet Union officials cannot disclose the exact figures for the grain harvest over the past two years, because they are still counting, said Mr Pyotr Paska, the Deputy Planning Minister.

7 High interest rates are bad for businesses because they have to pay more for loans.

Unit 5 What is a bank?

Preparing to read

Surveying before reading

A 1 A bank borrows and lends money for profit, looks after people's money, keeps accounts, transfers payments, gives financial advice, supplies cash to account-holders, stores valuables in its vaults, creates money by making loans . . .

B 1 its economic functions

D He is trying to do 2 and 4.

The passage

C 1 c

2 money

3 leave

4 employee

5 presumably, because the farmers had buried their money

6 the Thai Farmers' Bank
7 cash
8 a safe
9 on the farmers' deposits
10 the farmers' savings
11 interest
12 money
13 So banks are not just . . .
14 surplus
15 drains, water, wet, tanks, reservoirs
16 distributes it
17 what they had borrowed from the East Anglian farmers
18 the North of England
19 keeping money
20 mops up
21 cash
22 of the banks' total assets
23 With inflation, the value of cash goes down. Also the cost of keeping it is a drain on resources, and notes and coins have to be replaced because they get worn out. This adds to the cost of the banking system.
24 cash
25 the banking system
26 cash

What does the passage say?

A 1 It's a place where you keep money.
   2 b
   3 He got the farmers drunk.
   4 by offering them interest
   5 lent it out to other businesses at a higher rate of interest
   6 storage, drainage, irrigation and domestic water supply
   7 The reservoir must always have sufficient to supply farmers, factories and households.
   8 Cash earns no interest and is expensive to maintain.

Analysis

Logical link words

A 1 c   3 e   5 b   B 1 c   3 f   5 b
   2 c   4 d   6 a   2 e   4 a   6 d

Writing sentences

B 1 It is the cashier's job to pay out and receive the customers' money, keeping a record of all transactions.
   2 It is the banking system's function to absorb funds in areas of surplus, making them available in areas of deficit/need.
   3 It is the accountant's responsibility to meet customers at the counter, making sure that any problems are solved correctly.
   4 It is the security clerk's concern to examine securities received by the manager from customers, ensuring that they cover the bank's advances.

5 It is the statement's function to display all transactions, enabling customers to monitor their accounts.
6 It is the foreign clerk's job to help customers about to go abroad, providing them with travellers' cheques and foreign currency.
7 It is the remittance clerk's job to sort out cheques and credits paid in by customers, dividing them up according to the banks they are drawn on.
8 It is the money market's function to stabilise the exchange rates, providing a place where demand and supply can meet.
9 It is the clearing system's function to account for all receipts and payments in the country, totalling all credits and debits between the banks.
10 It is the central bank's responsibility to advise the government, executing its monetary policy.

C 1 By raising interest rates, the government tries to control the money supply.
   2 By making easy loans available, the World Bank encourages development.
   3 By borrowing from a merchant bank, the company obtains specialised advice.
   4 By providing financial support to agriculture, they hope to make the country self-sufficient in food.
   5 By keeping the amount of cash to a minimum, the banking system achieves big economies.

D   Discussion: (possible examples) The manager might agree to the loan, if I talk to her. We might open a restaurant in the old bank building. (possible intention) It might not be possible for them to get away before first light.

Extension

Tabulating notes

A 1 Table 1 just shows a list of the contents of each paragraph in the order they come. Table 2 divides up the subject matter into two main collections of points – a useful way of collecting notes if you have to write an essay on customer services and the banking system. Table 3 divides up the passage along the lines of the four major banking functions and looks at the passage as an explanation of the economic functions of banking.

Accurate use of words

   1 cash, withdrawals
   2 incentive, deposit, surplus wealth
   3 effectively   5 effective
   4 efficient   6 reserves

Further practice with words

A 1 this   3 which
   2 question   4 So/Therefore

5 borrower
6 lenders
7 But
8 honesty/reliability
9 also
10 his
11 If
12 his
13 the

14 He
15 information
16 If
17 it
18 private individuals/
   customers
19 and
20 expenditure
21 However
22 information

Self-assessment

A 1 a false   b true   c false
   2 a It is a bank manager's function to ensure that
      the work in his branch is going forward
      smoothly, checking and helping his staff at work.
      b It is a night security guard's work to make
      sure the bank is secure when it is otherwise
      empty, going round the building and checking all
      the doors and windows.   c One of the
      functions of a central bank is to ensure that the
      value of the national currency is maintained,
      buying and selling it in the money markets and
      retaining adequate reserves.
   3 I could put money into a long-term deposit
      account. This would attract a high interest rate.
      On the other hand, it might be better to place it
      in a current account so that I can withdraw it at
      any time.
   4 a reserves   b efficient
   5 a . . . lending at a higher rate of interest than
      the rate paid to depositors.   b . . . liquid
      resources and make them available to industry.
      (NOTE   Other answers are possible. If your
      answers are different, check them with your
      teacher.)

Unit 6 Banking problems:
Question analysis and
the reader's purpose

Preparing to answer questions

Topic analysis
A 1 c   2 e   3 b   4 d   5 a

Question functions
B 13 g   16 i   19 j   22 k
   14 f   17 c   20 d   23 a
   15 b   18 h   21 e

D 1 plan, report, enumerate
   2 enumerate, define, clarify
   3 clarify, explain, enumerate
   4 enumerate, define, inform
   5 clarify, define, summarise

6 inform, enumerate, summarise
   (NOTE   Many other functions could be used for
   these questions, but these are the most
   important ones.)

Choosing the right reply
B 3 f   5 e   7 k   9 d   11 g
   4 l   6 i   8 j   10 h   12 c

Analysis

Language
C 1 reasoning   6 reporting
   2 identifying   7 announcing
   3 hypothesising   8 comparing
   4 planning   9 summarising
   5 conceding   10 appreciating

Extension

Inference
B 1 Money can be taken out of the country without
      permission.
   2 I expect he will have the sense to leave any large
      amounts of money at home.
   3 You have to insist on payment in advance.
   4 It is not surprising that the first comprehensive
      banking law was introduced in Britain in 1979.

D 1 . . . is bad.
   2 . . . are passing on more of their costs to their
      customers.
   3 You should always check your bank statement.
      or Even banks can make mistakes.
   4 . . . had no effect on the money supply.
      (NOTE   Other sentences are possible; consult
      your English instructor.)

E c . . . you would have to wait longer before you
      stopped paying interest on an overdrawn
      account. (or, . . . started receiving interest on a
      new deposit account.)   d . . . being robbed/
      mugged/assaulted.   e . . . return cheques to
      the drawer.   f . . . the country of its
      customers . . . exchange.   g . . . £10,000.

G 1 b   2 a   3 b, c and d all apply

Self-assessment

A 1 given
   2 function
   3 purpose
   4 strategies
   5 on the dust-jacket (in the blurb)
   6 on the back of the title page
   7 c
   8 false
   9 true
   10 b
   11 a
   12 c

Unit 7 The creation of money

Preparing to read

Surveying the SCOPE
A 2 Banks create money by granting loans.
3 Yes, but only in a small proportion to the total money being created.
4 No.
5 Money created by granting credit or giving loans.
6 There are various ways of increasing the money supply: by increased borrowing, bank lending is increased; the government can also influence borrowing by raising or lowering interest rates; but, since 1945, there has been a tendency for the amount of money in the economy to increase whatever the banks and the government do.

B 1 Theory, section 2
2 historical and banking

C 1 It was not like any known animal and so could not be limited to a known animal's virtues. It could be given magic and mysterious powers which would be an advantage for a business.
2 earning interest
3 the original sum of capital lent or invested
4 A pair of scales to weigh coins, coins, moneybags, a seal, hammer and other items can be recognised.

The passage

D 1 rising up
2 He wanted to show that there were other non-physical media of exchange.
3 The inference is that paper money might have seemed unrelated to gold and that the time would come when notes would not give title to gold.
4 carried out
5 total withdrawals minus total deposits
6 b
7 thought about
8 keeping
9 safe-keeping
10 poor
11 charging a very high rate of interest
12 c
13 'it is worth pausing to spell out in more detail . . .'
14 b   15 a
16 assets
17 a liability of the goldsmiths' customers
18 £1,000   19 £1,000
20 assets
21 No.
22 the process of creating bank money
23 banknotes
24 a   25 pay

Discussion

D 1 true   2 false   3 false   4 true

E 1 liabilities   3 deposits   5 gold   7 £1,200
2 assets   4 bullion   6 certificates 8 £1,200

Analysis

Expressing sequence
C 1 decide   3 is   5 when   7 After
2 if   4 you   6 your   8 book

D 1 Until   3 From   5 When   7 buyer
2 gold   4 became   6 he

E 3 subject: Modern banking; verb: began
4 subject: the combined balance sheet of goldsmiths; verb: would be
5 subject: the likelihood; verb: is
6 subject: the balance sheet; verb: would be

F 1 During/At the time of/Following . . .
2 As time went on . . .
3 Following/At the time of . . .
4 Towards the end of . . .
5 When . . .
6 when . . .

Subordinate clauses
B 1 started/began, the goldsmiths
2 gave
3 became
4 were
5 would be paid
6 would be paid
7 he would reduce
8 that interest rates would be raised
9 the country's problems would be solved
10 the goods could be returned.
(NOTE   Other answers are possible. Check with your teacher.)

Extension

Note-making practice
B   Questions on 'Confidence without Gold':
1 banknotes
2 Reference words (line nos. are in brackets): *he* (5) refers to *Every banker* (3); *its* (14) to *every bank* (13); *it* (25) to *one bank of unquestioned solidity* (23–24); *this* (27) to *support the rest of the financial system* (24); *this* (28) to *the Bank of England* (27–28); *their* (31) to *the other banks* (30); *this* (33) to *the other banks gradually ceased to hold gold and centralized their reserves in the Bank of England* (30–32); *no serious adverse consequences* (50) to *crashes* (48); *paper money* (55) to *notes* (53); *it* (59) to *money* (59)
3 confidence of the customers
4 pay back

5 (ll. 16–17) '. . . there were a number of quite spectacular financial crashes'
6 periods of acute lack of trust
7 *all*
8 Even
9 illiquid
10 *Bankruptcy* occurs when total liabilities exceed total assets. *Illiquidity* occurs when there is not enough cash to pay debts.
11 At that time gold was thought to be the real money and if there was a crisis people who had banknotes or deposits in banks would rush to convert them into gold. It was therefore important for the bank concerned to be able to sell some of its assets for gold to meet the demand of its customers.
12 the Bank of England (ll. 27–28)
13 No. The concept of a Central Bank had not been realised, although the Bank of England fulfilled many of the roles of a central bank.
14 the public (not actually mentioned in the text, but see *depositors* (l. 11) and *People* (l. 38))
15 their banknotes issued by the bank in question
16 unfavourable
17 stopped temporarily   **19** varied
18 assets   **20** loans

C   (Model notes on text)
1 prudent/careful/cautious
2 serious/severe
3 keeps/kept/retains/retained
4 crashes/crises
5 bankruptcy   **9** banks
6 for   **10** gold/cash/liquid
7 be   **11** was
8 buy/cash/purchase **12** it

Self-assessment

A **1 b**
2 Subject, Coverage, Organisation, Purpose, Examples and illustrations
3 c
4 a
5 a
6 a When   **b** Then   **c** When
7 a With the increasing use of convertible paper money, many banks found it difficult to pay gold on demand.   **b** While many banks were facing liquidity problems, the need for a central bank became clear.
8 a Customers must be confident that their banks can pay cash on demand.   **b** . . . This means that capital reserves must not be expanded at the expense of leaving too few liquid assets.
9 a During the crisis people suspected that their banks could not pay gold for all the notes they had issued.   **b** They received a letter from their bank telling them that their overdraft had exceeded the limit agreed.

Unit 8 Graphs and tables

Reading graphs and tables

Comparing figures
A **1** invisible trade
2 1970–1   **3** 1980–1   **4** 1979–80
5 b
6 c The deteriorations were caused by the steep oil price increases.

B   smaller

Information from tables
A **1** In 1969–70 the trade gap decreased by 3,835.9 million rupees to 1,688.3 rupees.
2 In 1970–1 the trade gap decreased by 697.9 million rupees to 990.4 million rupees.
3 In 1971–2 the trade gap increased by 1,172.8 million rupees to 2,163.2 million rupees.
4 In 1972–3 there was a trade surplus of 1,033.9 million rupees.
5 In 1976–7 the trade gap of 12,220 million rupees was turned into a surplus of 720 million rupees.
6 In 1978–9 the trade gap increased by 4,670 million rupees to 10,880 million rupees.
7 In 1973–4, the trade surplus of the previous year was turned into a deficit of 4,359.7 million rupees.
8 In 1976–7 the trade deficit of the previous year was turned into a surplus of 720 million rupees.

B **1** In 1965–6 imports exceeded exports by 6,028.8 million rupees.
2 In 1972–3 exports exceeded imports by 1,033.9 million rupees.
3 In 1976–7 exports exceeded imports by 720 million rupees.

C **1** The trade gap narrowed in 1969–70 by 3,835.9 million rupees to 1,688.3 million rupees.
2 In 1971–2 the trade gap widened by 1,172.8 million rupees to 2,163.2 million rupees.
3 In 1979–80 the trade gap widened by 13,610 million rupees to 24,490 million rupees.

Understanding graphs
B **1** Rupees
2 d
3 a true **b** true **c** true **d** false **e** true **f** false
4 It is easier to get an overall *visual* impression of the trading position over the period shown by the table.
5 It gives more precise information on figures than a graph.

Information from graphs
1 In the year 1975–6 imports levelled off while exports rose steadily, producing a small trade surplus.

2 In the year 1976–7 imports showed a slight decrease while exports rose sharply, producing a small trade surplus.

3 In the year 1977–8 imports climbed steadily while exports levelled off, producing a growing trade deficit.

4 In the year 1980–1 imports climbed steeply whilst exports increased only slightly, producing a huge trade deficit.

More on graphic information

A   1 B   3 A   5 D   7 A   9 C
   2 D   4 C   6 B   8 A   10 D

B   1 1,720,000   2 1978   3 1980 & 1981
   4 Yes, because at the bottom of Table A it says KDs are included in Toyota's production.
   5 Toyota has succeeded in raising production every year except 1974.
   6 1980
   7 GM–1974, Ford–1980, VW–1974, Toyota–1974

C   1 North America   3 The EEC   5 1,711,000
   2 91,000   4 Europe

D   1 8.7%   2 The Near and Middle East   3 4.7%

E   1 41,020,000
   2 an increase of 13,140,000 cars
   3 Africa
   4 North America
   5 Africa and The Near and Middle East

Writing from graphs and tables

A report

A   1 3,333,000   10 Near and Middle East
   2 second   11 Asia
   3 overseas   12 18,740,000
   4 41,020,000   13 14,030,000
   5 3,073,000   14 manufacturers
   6 ten (10)   15 1978
   7 USA   16 Toyota
   8 692,456   17 Southeast Asia
   9 Europe   18 2,100,000

B   (Correct but less acceptable words are shown in brackets.)
   1 DBS   4 11,271.1   7 OCBC
   2 growing   5 Banking   8 Singapore
   3 OCBC   6 DBS   9 103.09   10 UOB
   11 net: You can tell this from the note at the bottom of the table which says the figures are after tax.
   12 OUB
   13 team (group)
   14 innovative (aggressive, inventive, imaginative, advanced)
   15 several (many, numerous)
   16 leader (master)
   17 Singapore
   18 celebrates (commemorates)
   19 price, penalty
   20 UOB
   21 improvements (growth, increases, advances)
   22 OUB   23 OCBC   24 UOB
   25 However (Nevertheless)
   26 top, first (foremost, leading)

Further writing from tables

Writing about exports

A   The figures for the last twenty to thirty years show an overall decline in agricultural exports. On the one hand there has been a steady fall in the exports of the five leading commodities. In addition, the contribution to exports in value of eight major products has almost disappeared. In general, one can say that Nigeria has changed from being a major agricultural exporting country to being one which now exports comparatively little.

A detailed examination of the figures clarifies what has happened. In 1960 the contribution of major crops was 76.7% of exports. In 1980 this was reduced to 2.4%. The biggest fall came between 1960 and 1968 when the share of agricultural commodities fell from 76.7% to only 30.9% representing a drop of over 40%. Thereafter, agricultural exports decreased steadily to 1980.

Export volumes, however, present an interesting contrast to the rather gloomy percentage contributions to total exports. Although there was a general decline in output of the five leading products, there were several peak years. For cocoa these were in 1971, 1976 and 1979. For palm kernels 1946, 1971 and 1976 were peak years. Groundnuts and groundnut oil exports were also substantial in the early seventies.

So, in conclusion, it can be said that exports of agricultural commodities have declined in volume over the past thirty-four years. But the contribution of agricultural products to total exports has declined more rapidly than actual export volume. For example, cocoa exports in 1980 were higher than they were in the 1940s, but their share of total exports value had fallen in the period 1960–80 to 2.2% from 22.2%.

Self-assessment

A   1 a exceed   b slowly/gradually/slightly, fast/rapidly/quickly   c by, to
   2 bar graph, pie chart, tables of figures, line graph
   3 line graph
   4 pie chart
   5 bar graph
   6 a sharp   b slow   c trough   d rise
   e uncertain   f upturn   g collapse
   h deficit
   (NOTE   Other words are possible. Consult your teacher.)

Unit 9 The origins of central banking

Preparing to read

Surveying before reading

A 1 A central bank is the chief government bank in the country.
2 It supervises the other banks and the banking system; it keeps government accounts and reserves; it carries out government monetary policy; it is the bankers' bank, keeping accounts and reserves of other banks. (This is a short list. One can go into more detail.)
3 It is government owned. (The Bank of England was a private company for 255 years and was nationalised in 1949.)
7 c
8 Central banks are needed by their governments to raise money and help to carry out economic policy. (A short answer: there is much more to say on this question.)
9 The central bank is a public institution and is responsible to the country as a whole, while a commercial bank is a business and is intended to make profits for its owners.

B 2 **a** the seventeenth to the eighteenth century
b Amsterdam's **c** £1,340,000 **d** France, Holland, Germany, Sweden, Canada, Scotland
4 **a** the centre of world trade **b** Wisselbank
c trade **d** 1694

C 1 The larger text is about financial economics in Europe from 1500–1730.
2 This passage deals with the economic factors leading to the development of government banks.
3 The last paragraph summarises the reasons for the survival of the Bank of England in contrast with the decline of other financial experiments.

D 1 There is a large amount of historical reporting, but the main purpose of the passage is to interpret and generalise about events.

E 1 It is a group of banking centres in different places which keep accounts for each other. (See *nostra* and *vostra* accounts in your textbooks.)
2 He wanted to show that Amsterdam had more connections than London in financial terms.
3 The Baltic regions, Eastern Europe and Turkey.
4 Yes. It had connections with Florence and Rome in Italy and the British colonies in America.

The passage

B 1 exchange banks (l. 7)
2 because 'total issue of deposit certificates never exceeded the total bullion held in the bank'
3 local government
4 Germany, Holland, Sweden 5 these/those

6 it 7 undisputed
8 clearing-house (ll. 5–6)
9 superiority
10 *Seaside* is used in the context of holidays (Brighton is a seaside resort). *Coastal* is used in physical geography when you are thinking of land (coastal waters, coastal cities). *Maritime* means that the people of the city were seafarers and ocean traders.
11 This
12 credit instrument
13 paid
14 Bills of Exchange used to finance trade
15 in Amsterdam
16 commanding . . . position
17 its 18 the octopus
19 ascendancy
20 shows
21 exchange
22 were
23 accepting Bills of Exchange (l. 28)
24 off, her (England's)
25 set off . . . against
26 that of Amsterdam
27 them
28 exchange dealings
29 British trade
30 No.
31 it
32 to pay for the war in France (see l. 41)
33 By 1698, By 1720
34 all forms of paper money (e.g. banknotes, gold certificates, promissory notes, Bills of Exchange)
35 The Bank of England was set up as a business to exploit the government's need. (The Wisselbank was more in the nature of a public service utility.) The Bank also issued 'running cash notes' and carried out a variety of banking activities for the government.
36 25%
37 *specie* = gold & silver. Because the Wisselbank never issued more notes than it had gold in its vaults, these notes were regarded as 100b safe.
38 The Wisselbank was unable to expand the money supply to meet the needs of commerce, because of its rule never to issue more notes than the amount of gold it had.
39 was
40 sank
41 1500–1730
42 became established
43 in America (what is now the USA)
44 Yes, but not at face value. 45 their

Analysis

Word study

1 d	4 p	7 i	10 a	13 k	16 c
2 g	5 b	8 j	11 e	14 n	
3 o	6 h	9 l	12 m	15 f	

Combining sentences

B 1 The Bank of England, founded as a joint-stock company in 1694, was at the centre of the new-found prosperity.

2 At first the Bank only issued notes known as 'running cash notes', but later it went on to provide a great many other services to the government.

3 The innovations introduced at the end of the seventeenth century enabled the money supply to be increased by 25% without increasing the amount of cash.

4 Experiments with paper money promoted in Sweden and France foundered because notes exceeded gold by too large a margin.

5 The cheque signed by the managing director got lost in the post and so it had to be cancelled.

6 To avoid delay, shipping documents, made out exactly as stated in the credit, should be forwarded to the bank as soon as possible.

7 Cheques, supported by bank cards, should be made payable to Universal Stores Ltd.

8 Recently the practice of returning cheques drawn by account holders with monthly statements was discontinued by many banks.

Listing

B (example) The clearing banks offer a range of services to personal customers: running current and deposit accounts, making credit transfers, providing regular statements, carrying out standing order payments, making travellers' cheques available and changing foreign currency.

Phrasal verbs

B 1 Should we accept this cheque, drawn on an unknown bank?

2 One is allowed to set off (offset) normal business expenses against taxation.

3 profited from   **4** based on   **5** expanded . . . by
6 to trade in   **7** accepted at
8 was built up (intended as, founded as)
9 exceeded by   **10** redeemed at

Extension

Generalisation

B Para. 3: The secret of Amsterdam's ascendancy lay in the ubiquity of Dutch trading concerns. (l. 18) Evidence: Dutch merchants everywhere, Bills could be drawn on Amsterdam everywhere, large bullion reserves, stable exchange rates, many exchange connections . . . Para. 4: Amsterdam's position only weakened when London's trade overtook it (mainly after 1713). Evidence: commodity trade, exchange dealings became as big as Amsterdam's (delay in catching up caused by war with France) Para. 5: The Bank of England was at the centre of the new prosperity. Evidence: successful loans to the

government, numerous other services; financial innovations enabled the money supply to be increased without increase of specie . . . Para. 6: Creation of money by the Bank of England was uniquely successful. Evidence: Wisselbank notes restricted to gold deposits, Swedish and French experiments foundered because too many notes were issued, limited successs of banknotes in North America . . .

Main and contributory factors
1 b   **2 c**   **3 c**   **4 b**   **5 a**

Self-assessment

A 1 b & d
2 a Skimming is running your eyes over the text to give yourself a general idea of what the text is about.   **b** It helps to skim a text before reading it in detail because the added familiarity with the subject matter will help you to understand and learn the contents better.
c When you skim you usually notice names, dates and sums of money, along with anything printed differently (e.g. in italics, block capitals, bold – heavy black – type).
3 a   **4** credit instrument   **5 b**
6 The company set up last year has already gone bankrupt.
7 based on
8 details (evidence, facts)

Unit 10 The origins of central banking

Preparing to read

Surveying before reading

A 1 The end of the seventeenth century.
2 Amsterdam, covering maritime cities all over the world.
3 increasing world trade, influx of bullion, severe shortages of money (esp. in time of war)
4 It was situated in London, which was about to overtake Amsterdam in volume of trade; also it mastered the art of issuing notes in the right proportion to its gold reserves.

B 1 Information in the first two lines of each paragraph: King Charles II was having financial problems. He was trying to solve them in an unpopular way. Under the next king things were little better.
2 Some events and dates: 1671 the 'Stop of the Exchequer', 1685 death of Charles II, 1689 war with France, 1689–1702 government expenditure was £72 m, April 1694 the loan which founded the Bank of England was floated . . .

3 Some sums of money: loan of 1671 which the king failed to repay was £2,250,000; 1693 loan £1,000,000, etc.

D 1 The government needed money badly; an expensive war with France had started; several unsuccessful attempts had been made to solve the problem; there was plenty of money about in London.

2 The Wisselbank declined mainly because it didn't attempt to become a bank of issue but remained only a depository. Another reason was that the Dutch were not doing so well as the English economically.

3 The other banks usually over-issued notes and crashed when people started demanding gold in exchange for them. The Bank of England avoided this situation.

E 1 Although the Bank was a large, powerful and rich national institution, it was happy to use a rather humble looking building as an address. This seems to show that the Dutch did not favour display of wealth.

2 It was important to be next to the town hall since the Corporation of Amsterdam was a major customer; probably directors of the bank were also members of the municipality.

The passage

1 King of the UK 1649–85
2 his predecessors
3 rulers who came before
4 towards the improvement of Charles II's finances
5 promising to solve the financial problem
6 were   7 Finance   8 accumulated
9 Amsterdam was the most successful financial centre in the world at that time.
10 London   11 seethed
12 to the problem of the government's inability to pay its debt
13 Stop   14 direct   15 payment
16 the 'Stop of the Exchequer'
17 orders temporarily not repaid
18 alteration
19 original capital
20 desperately, surer footing
21 Charles II
22 clear, consistent
23 members of the government
24 William III's
25 several years
26 convenient methods
27 money before they received it
28 No.   29 yearly payment
30 interest   31 money product
32 to the 'perpetual' loan of January 1693
33 idea
34 people who provided the capital
35 set up   36 Exchequer

Analysis

Statement and implication

B Underlined words should be:
1 was only recognised
2 refused to recognise
3 only . . . under
4 further long-term loans followed (Note the use of *a* in *a lottery was launched* and *a loan . . . was invited.*)
5 carried the ministers . . . through

Writing sentences

B 1 The proceeds of taxation were anticipated by long-term loans.
2 Only 10% of the cost of the war was financed by long-term loans.
3 The first of these 'perpetual' loans, which was floated in 1693, was guaranteed by Parliament.
4 The principle of government long-term borrowing was introduced for the first time by the life annuity fund of 1693.
5 In March £1,000,000 was raised by the city through a lottery.
6 A loan of £1.2 million was then invited in April.
7 Interest payments were suspended by the government in 1685 and the debt was only recognised in 1707.
8 Several branches in the country were opened by the National Bank last year.
9 A large loan for the government was approved by the IMF on condition that taxation was increased.
10 Massive cutbacks in government spending were announced by the Chancellor.

D 1 e   2 d   3 c   4 b   5 a

E (examples)
1 Without wishing to exaggerate, I would say the manager was guilty of complete neglect.
2 On the positive side, he did try to make good the loss.
3 Even more important, he was finally able to trace the error.
4 From the account holder's point of view, the bank settled the matter fairly.

G (examples)
1 Sugar-production, the mainstay of . . .
2 Mr Kinnock, the Leader of the Opposition, gave details of . . .
3 The Tapioca Bay Project, funded by the Asian Development Bank, . . . $4 million.
4 Mr Goldworthy, the governor . . ., announced an increase in . . .

Complex sentences

1 According to the Bank Negara's latest quarterly Economic Bulletin, economic activity in the second quarter of 1982 continued to be dampened by the prolonged recession.

2 Reflecting weak international demand for primary commodities, gross export earnings stagnated at the level of the corresponding quarter of 1981.

3 Except for palm oil and palm kernels, production of other major commodities declined.

4 While manufacturing output recovered moderately, mining production remained relatively strong due to increased oil production.

5 Aggregate domestic demand in the second quarter was generally sustained by continued moderate growth in private sector expenditure and a sharp rise in public sector spending.

6 Imports of consumer goods continued to increase at an annual rate of 11.5%, although this was slower than the 32.4% growth in the corresponding quarter of 1981.

Extension

Formal language in banking

1 Conversion
2 management, instruments
3 froze, suspended
4 floated, issue, oversubscribed
5 endorse   6 budget deficit

Self-assessment

A 1 Skim the first lines of each paragraph and note any prominent items, such as sums of money, that catch your eye.
2 Ask yourself certain questions on information you want to know before you start reading.
3 b   4 c   5 c
6 a Chancellor b spread c deficit d suspended
7 imply, implication
8 a They launched a new loan at 7% a few years later.   b A variety of important services was provided by the new bank.   c Clearly, the bank was in trouble early in January.
d Megaprom, the well-known import agents, were appointed by the bank as receiving agents.

Unit 11 Banking and development

Preparing to read and write

How content of texts is organised

C 1 unofficial   4 rules   7 b
2 formal   5 home-grown   8 b
3 impersonal   6 a

Question analysis and note-making

B   (question functions)
1 review the situation of rural credit, analyse the problems, suggest solutions, use reason to

support your suggestions, reject some possibilities . . .
2 define multi-agency approach, enumerate and analyse the problems, suggest how they could be solved . . .
3 evaluate or judge, enumerate (instances of where private sector banking can contribute) . . .
4 explain with reasoning, enumerate and justify your selection of banking functions . . .

The passage

C 1 unorganised sector
2 joint-stock banks   3 long-term
4 The commercial banks were public companies with shareholders from the public, whilst traditional sector banks were operated by their owners. Also the commercial banks were larger and more formal.
5 in goods   6 50–70%
7 The money-lenders   a grant consumer credit b operate with their own capital, and c do not deal with hundis and have no access to the financial market.
8 legal features   9 in use
10 permitted delay   11 dashani
12 people or companies   13 dekhaner jog
14 It isn't used for foreign trade; the form of wording varies from place to place; the Bill of Exchange is not normally used for inland trade.
15 This is the period of farm production and trade in produce.
16 by merchants
17 for obtaining cash when they need it (normally in exchange for Treasury Bills or other short-term assets)
18 If they are short of cash they rely on the commercial banks to rediscount their hundis (see ll. 62–65)
19 the link between the commercial banks and the Central Bank
20 the regulation of the Income Tax Act mentioned in line 90

E   (Questions on the organisation of the passage)
1 inductive
2 Hundi business is largely independent of the organised sector.
3 deductively
4 the stability of interest rates up to 1973
5 They do not contradict the main point that the hundi sector is largely unaffected by the official banking system. The hundi market was upset by other factors than the Central Bank regulations.

Discussion

Ask and answer

A 1 & 2 indigenous banking and money lending

3 lending to the princely states

4 No, because the traditional bankers do not as a rule lend for consumer purchases.

5 promissory note, but it doesn't have all its legal features

6 business loans, agricultural produce loans, goods in trade, transfers of cash assets; but they aren't used for international transactions or consumer purchases

7 It rediscounts hundis.

8 No.

9 flexible, easy to arrange, informal, reliable

10 cheap, convenient, efficient; and the hundi can be discounted in the local money market

12 It can change the minimum lending rate and affect the interest rates in the hundi sector indirectly. The rate will also be affected by the availability of liquidity.

13 In the 1970s the hundi discount rates remained fairly stable while the money market rates fluctuated.

14 & **15** risk of coming under government control, no consumer credit available (you still have to go to a bank or other institution for a house mortgage, or to buy a car), not able to finance foreign trade

17 & **18** They operate in the market on a person-to-person basis, while in a modern bank one would deal with an official over the counter; loans can be obtained quickly and informally while in a bank one would probably have to complete forms, make out a case for the loan and present accounts; traditional banker deals are more secretive.

19 They made a rule that all payments over Rs. 2,500 had to be made by draft or crossed cheque.

20 The regulation made it compulsory for all payments over Rs. 2,500 to be made by draft or crossed cheque in order to be acceptable to the tax authorities. This meant that all hundis for that sum or more were illegal from the tax point of view.

Analysis

Omitting 'which' and 'that'

B Sentences **1**, **3**, **4**, **5** and **7** can omit **which**. Sentences **2**, **6** and **8** cannot omit *which*.

Using 'can be . . .ed'

B **1** . . . demarcation can be drawn . . .
   2 . . . business can be carried on . . .
   3 . . . business can be transacted . . .
   4 . . . services can be easily integrated with . . .

Opening phrase with 'as'

B **1** As in many other countries . . .
   2 As can be seen by anyone who examines the facts . . .

3 As my bank manager knows . . .

4 As is undoubtedly the case . . .

Expressing concession

B **1** Although the interest rates were high, people still borrowed money.

   2 In spite of high interest rates, the money supply increased as fast as ever.

   3 While there was considerable demand for the car, sales remained at a low level.

   4 In spite of their important role in financing the movement of agricultural produce, loans to agriculture were only 3.5% of the total credit.

   5 Although indigenous bankers tend to be concentrated in urban areas, they fulfil a vital function in areas where commercial banks are unrepresented. (or Although they fulfil . . .)

Extension

Use of vocabulary

C **1** described as
   2 distinguished from
   3 is lent on
   4 are determined by
   5 provide each other with
   6 deals mainly in
   7 concentrated so much in
   8 distinguish between
   9 consist of
   10 deal directly with
   11 was taken over
   12 lend in
   13 concerned with
   14 uses them for   **15** rediscount the Bills with

E **1** inherent in   **5** apart from
   2 similar to   **6** payable on
   3 dependent on   **7** payable at
   4 questionable whether

G **1** access to   **3** three days' grace
   2 connection between   **4** In contrast with

Self-assessment

A **1** a   **3** b   **5** a   **7** a
   2 a   **4** b   **6** c

   8 a A study of the traditional rural credit systems used in India may help us to . . .

   9 can be obtained

   10 Although modern banks have spread to most parts of the country . . .

   11 Despite the advanced nature of the financial system the problem . . .

   12 The traditional bankers are dependent on the joint-stock banks to rediscount their hundis if they are short of cash/money/liquidity/funds. So there is a connection with the national banking system. Apart from this, however, the public sector banks do not normally deal with hundis.

Unit 12 Banking and development

Preparing to read and write

Organising topics
A 1 Economic Development

B 2 responsibility
3 investment banking
4 agricultural credit
5 industrial development banking
6 project evaluation
7 credit security
8 modernisation of agriculture
9 mechanisation of agriculture

Reading and making notes
B Topics (Note that complete lists of topics cannot be given here, so you may wish to add your own topics.)
1 agricultural credit and   **a** economic development   **b** modernisation
c mechanisation   **d** improving standards of living   **e** public vs. private sector credit
f credit security   **g** cash crop production vs. national self-sufficiency in food
2 the role of the middleman and his possible replacement: **a** functions of the middleman
b advantages and disadvantages of middleman dealing   **c** rural debt   **d** two commodities and their characteristic production and marketing problems and benefits   **e** the difference between middleman dealing and bank dealing
3 development banking: **a** social responsibility vs. financial responsibility   **b** national interest vs. personal or local interest   **c** industrial development   **d** agricultural development
e project evaluation   **f** political influences
g the difference between commercial banking and development banking

Reading passage A

B 1 independence
2 one solution would be . . ., could be given . . ., perhaps under an installment payment basis . . .
3 the establishment of multi-purpose joint-stock companies
4 government land
5 legal ownership   6 fair
7 in order to introduce modern methods of agriculture, protect the interests of the peasants and demonstrate the advantages of modernisation
8 the main purpose of the tripartite agreement
9 the joint-stock company
10 because farming hasn't acquired a respectable image

11 (l. 19) . . . with the provision that, if the land is neglected, the joint stock company would take possession of the land . . .
12 (l. 19) absolute title
13 He uses the words 'Somewhat similar schemes could be introduced . . .'
14 a joint-stock company
15 put together
16 workable
17 the government
18 to get work when there is no work to be done on the land
19 rewards
20 for the reasons that

Reading passage B

B 1 small – great
2 the imbalance between the financial needs and the actual flow of investment
3 collect
4 urban
5 Three: injecting into rural areas funds raised
a in urban areas   **b** from foreign loans
c from taxation
6 (see Unit 4, **Formality**) The inverted commas show that the writer is aware that the expression is too informal for this text but he has chosen to use it in this case to avoid a long explanation.
7 resolution
8 inductive
9 Problem of rural financial needs in development:
a past investment failures, lack of govt understanding of
i) long-term nature of the investment   and
ii) lack of quick return
b What is needed is:
i) finance from outside the ag. sector
ii) a 'hard' banking attitude
– otherwise money will be wasted   and
– one needs to impress on peasants the true value of capital
Note the importance of a clear layout for easy revision (See Unit 10, **Note-making**)
10 business-like, tough, firm, strict
11 lending on easy terms and interest less than the normal rates
12 waste in small amounts
13 It is the title of a government department.
14 It is a quotation.
15 of interest and capital repayments
16 bringing to an end
17 attack
18 the people of the country concerned
19 wave a magic wand and let people off their debts
20 necessary part of the whole
21 same
22 The agricultural credit banks should take over the functions of the traditional money-lender.
23 The writer is adapting the expression from Bills of Exchange.

24 discount
25 the use of Bills as credit instruments having a money value within the rural sector
26 'Any such scheme would require . . .'
27 It seems to be worth looking into this proposal./It would be worth studying this scheme in more detail.
28 a government marketing authority (l. 78)
29 invest
30 reluctance
31 to encourage investment in agriculture from within the country
32 the Bills of Exchange
33 of the bills, e.g. 30 days, 60 days or 120 days after sight
34 increased
35 'Of course, the proposal might be regarded simply as an extension of . . .'
36 not concrete
37 the government's
38 Nevertheless
39 at the same time
40 Parallel agricultural reforms are also necessary, such as land distribution, modernisation, mechanisation, changes in the rural infrastructure.

Discussion

Ask and answer

A 1 What sort of agricultural reforms could be carried out in a mixed economy? What are the problems of agricultural development in a mixed economy?
2 How could a joint-stock company participate in agricultural development?
3 What is land title? How can peasants be assured of the title to their land in a land reform scheme? How would land reform affect landowners' title to land?
4 What does 'in arrears' mean? What sort of debtors are likely to get into arrears?
5 What does 'wind up' mean?
6 What is 'maturity'? What might have a range of maturities? What are the advantages of a range of maturities?
7 What does 'credit-worthy' mean?
8 What does 'underwrite' mean?
9 What is a 'rural produce Bill'? What are the advantages of rural produce Bills compared with money-lenders as a way of financing agricultural production? How do rural produce Bills work? What drawbacks are there?
10 What is a bond? How is it used?
11 What does 'rural produce paper' mean?
12 What does 'domestic debt' refer to? (If in doubt how to answer, see the subject index of one of your textbooks.)

B **a** and **b**:
1 What is the national food production policy in . . .?
2 What are the main food imports/exports?
3 Do the private sector banks in . . . participate in agricultural credit?
4 Is small size of farm/peasant holdings a problem in . . .?
5 What is the government policy on land reform/modernisation/mechanisation/land distribution/co-operatives?
6 What is the role of the middleman in . . .?
7 Is there a land reform policy in . . .?
8 How successful is agricultural modernisation?
9 What are the advantages/disadvantages of mechanisation?
10 How is migration to the cities dealt with? How can migration to the cities be discouraged? What is the government's policy on migration to the cities?
11 (Use the same question form as No. 10.)
12 What is the state of agricultural production in . . .?

C Subjects to discuss: world food prices; growing export crops vs. crops for the domestic market; repayment of foreign debt; effect of importation of free food aid on local markets. Factors in international trade: poor grain harvests or shortages in a rich country (e.g. the USSR) drive up the prices of grain; conversely, grain surpluses mean a fall in prices and government subsidies to farmers in the US not to produce grain – also poorer grain producing countries (e.g. Argentina) lose heavily in export earnings; shipment of grain given by way of aid is usually harmful to the receiving country since its farmers are unable to produce and sell grain if free grain is being given away by the government; a major market for US grain is the EEC where it is used for animal fodder.

Analysis

Preparing to write

B 2 exchanged question
3 alteration of question
4 vague example
5 unnecessary restatement of the question
6 confusing the question with a separate issue

E 1 It will be necessary to arrange for a tripartite agreement among the government, the joint-stock company and the small landholder. Under this, modern methods of agriculture would be introduced where necessary by the company. It could thus demonstrate the advantages of these methods to the peasants.

2 The foregoing would apply to extensive land that is leased to joint-stock companies and to small lots sold outright to peasants who have title to them. The condition would be that the possession of the land would temporarily pass to appropriate joint-stock companies if it remains either undeveloped or underdeveloped.

3 In some countries large areas of government land have been taken over by capitalist groups and developed successfully. Such lands have been subsequently expropriated by socialist governments. The grounds for this were that the capitalists were exploiting the peasant community living around them.

Using the correct particle

1 necessary to
2 view loans as gifts
3 committed to
4 take possession of
5 hand it over in return for
6 would go a long way to ensuring
7 it would apply to
8 could be introduced in
9 could be allocated to
10 is engaged in
11 take on
12 injected into
13 for want of support
14 associated with
15 impress upon
16 suggest a way
17 compete with
18 provide the farmers with
19 take advantage of
20 a means of taking advantage of

Extension

Develop your word power

A 1 autonomy   7 participation
2 elaborate   8 enable
3 solution   9 permanent
4 neglected   10 adequate
5 modern   11 pool
6 safeguarded   12 capitalist groups

B 1 rendered
2 for want of sufficient government recognition of the difficulties involved in . . .
3 supplying agricultural credit
4 the consequent lack of resolution
5 to meet the needs of small-scale rural producers
6 requires access to savings from outside the agricultural sector as a major source of funds
7 improve the position of the rural cultivators
8 assist the small rural producers

C 1 diffuse
2 farmers
3 underwrite
4 caused by
5 paying debts
6 consider it important, feel obliged
7 additional benefits
8 there is a willingness/people are willing

Answering the question

B (NOTE   There are several ways of writing opening sentences for these questions. The following are examples only. Check your own examples with your English teacher.)

1 The main problem of agricultural credit is that lending to farmers is less profitable than lending in other sectors . . .
2 Let us take tomatoes and wheat as examples. The main difference is that, with the former, the middleman has to provide fast delivery to the customer, while the wheat middleman is concerned more with storage . . .
3 A development bank should provide finance which development projects need and which normal commercial banks are unwilling to supply . . .
4 The main reason for this is that greater profits can be made in areas other than in development.

Self-assessment

A 1 b and to some extent c
2 a true   b false   c false
3 a necessary   b This   c help/assist/finance
d Past/Elaborate/Government   e or/from
f they/governments   g They/Governments/Officials   h is   i on   j several/many
k demand/need   l sources/institutions
m have/need/want   n more   o The
p problem   q is   r basically/fundamentally
s losses   t purposes/aims   u strict/stringent/legalistic/normal   v will
w system/scheme/network/plan   x with
4 a difficulties in   b access to   c supervision of
5 a underwrite   b rediscounted   c bonds